Who's to Say?

Who's to Say?
A Dialogue on Relativism

Norman Melchert

Hackett Publishing Company, Inc.
Indianapolis/Cambridge

Copyright©1994 by Hackett Publishing Company, Inc.

Printed in the United States of America

00 99 98 97 96   3 4 5 6 7

For further information, please address

Hackett Publishing Company, Inc.
P.O. Box 44937
Indianapolis, Indiana 46244-0937

Design by Dan Kirklin

Library of Congress Cataloging-in-Publication Data

Melchert, Norman.
  Who's to say?: a dialogue on relativism/Norman Melchert.
      p.   cm.
  ISBN 0-87220-272-0 (hard: alk. paper).   ISBN 0-87220-271-2 (pbk.:
alk. paper)
    1. Ethical relativism. 2. Values. I. Title.
  BJ1031.M37 1994
  171'.7 – dc20   94-21086
                                                  CIP

The paper used in this publication meets the minimum requirements of
American National Standard for Information Sciences – Permanence of
Paper for Printed Library Materials, ANSI Z39.48-1984.

∞

for Novi

Author's Note

I am grateful to Lehigh University for a leave of absence, and to the University of Waikato, Hamilton, New Zealand, for making me welcome during the time I wrote this dialogue. I thank those who contributed to making this a better work, especially Gordon Bearn, Mark Bickhard, David Lumsden, Dennis Melchert, Matthew Melchert, and Paul Coppock.

Who's to Say?

Who's to Say?
A Dialogue on Relativism

FRED, the assistant manager of a BMW dealership

SAM, a dentist

ELIZABETH, a high-school math teacher

MICHAEL, a mechanical engineer working for a large multinational firm

ANITA, a lawyer

PETER, an assistant professor of English literature at a small midwestern college

* *

This is a record of conversations that occurred on three consecutive evenings. The six participants had been close friends while students at the university ten years earlier. Before they graduated, they vowed to get together in a decade. For their reunion, they chose a five-day summer bicycle tour in Vermont. As the first conversation opens, they are relaxing after dinner at an inn on the evening of their second day of cycling. Fred has just picked up a worn copy of Herodotus' *Histories* probably left at the inn by some student on an earlier tour.

* *

1

The First Conversation

The Evening of Their Second Day Together

FRED: Listen to this: "Everyone without exception believes his own native customs, and the religion he was brought up in, to be the best. . . . There is abundant evidence that this is the universal feeling about the ancient customs of one's country. One might recall, in particular, an anecdote of Darius. When he was king of Persia, he summoned the Greeks who happened to be present at his court, and asked them what they would take to eat the dead bodies of their fathers. They replied that they would not do it for any money in the world. Later, in the presence of the Greeks, and through an interpreter, so they could understand what was said, he asked some Indians, of the tribe called Callatiae, who do in fact eat their parents' dead bodies, what they would take to burn them. They uttered a cry of horror and forbade him to mention such a dreadful thing. One can see by this what custom can do, and Pindar, in my opinion, was right when he called it 'king of all.' " [1]

Now, isn't that just what I always used to say? Custom is king over all! And Herodotus already saw it clearly a couple of thousand years ago.

SAM: Yes, that's what you always said, all right. You said it too often, if you ask me! And I'm surprised you haven't learned better by now. Why, if *custom* is king over all, then there's no objective truth, no absolute good or evil, and no escape from what most people say. And those consequences are absurd.

FRED: Absurd? On the contrary, they're as obvious as anything can be. Don't you remember our anthropology course? You may be horrified when you find cultures that expose old people to starvation or strangle them. But people who live in these cultures defend such practices; they think it would be cruel to leave elderly

1. Herodotus, *The Histories*, (Penquin Books, 1972), bk. 3, sec. 38.

3

parents to suffer the miseries of old age. Herodotus is right: each culture thinks its own practices are best.

SAM: *That* may be. But thinking so doesn't make it so.

ELIZABETH: Here's an idea. Why don't we agree to talk about this? We used to have some great discussions when we were together back at school. And it might be fun to sharpen our wits on each other again.

MICHAEL: Discussions, you say? They seemed like *arguments* to me.

ELIZABETH: Well, whatever you call them, they were sure interesting. And I've missed them. I think I learned a lot from talking to you all.

ANITA: I think Liz has a good idea. We caught up on personal and family lives last night. And we don't want to spend all the rest of our time talking about the weather.

PETER: Or the roads either. But speaking of them, wasn't that second hill today a killer? I almost got off and walked. I would have, too, except that I vowed I wouldn't do that this trip.

FRED: We'll see whether you can keep that vow, Peter. I understand the worst hills are still to come.

SAM: I'd welcome a chance to talk about this topic. I think it's important. And, if you want to know, conversations in a dentist's office aren't exactly stimulating.

PETER: It's hard to talk when someone has a hand in your mouth.

ELIZABETH: Are we agreed then? For the next several evenings we will examine the question: Is custom king over all?

ANITA: If I'm not mistaken, the view that custom is king has a name; it's called *relativism*. How shall we begin? I suspect this can get very involved.

MICHAEL: Why don't we start by asking why anybody would think that "everything's relative," as some people put it? What got

Herodotus going, apparently, was becoming aware of the *very* different ways people live in different places and times – the different judgments they make and their varied beliefs.

FRED: That's the main thing. He also noticed that despite the differences, people are always convinced *their* way is best.

ANITA: That's got a name, too. It's called *ethnocentrism*.

MICHAEL: Right. Well, I notice both of those things, the differences and the preference for one's own ways, when I go to Japan on business. I have to be careful to observe the local customs if I don't want to offend my prospective clients.

FRED: Well, there you are! Doesn't that settle it? This may be a very short conversation and not involved at all. Custom *is* king, and everyone does as the king says.

ANITA: It's not that simple, Fred. All we have noted so far is the fact of *diversity* – and the love people have for familiar ways. That's a long way from saying everything is relative.

MICHAEL: It's the "everything" that bothers me. In Japan I bow when I meet someone, I don't come directly to the point of my business, and I drive on the left side of the road. But those are things, I want to say, that don't really *matter*.

FRED: You just told us that they matter if you want to do business there! Or, I might add, if you want to avoid a car accident.

MICHAEL: I don't mean to deny they have a certain importance. But surely we can all agree that there are some things – these among them – which can be done equally well one way or another. When in Japan I do them the Japanese way, when at home in my own way. It's simply a matter of conforming to the prevailing custom, and it's no big deal. These things are relative to a culture, and properly so.

SAM: "When in Rome . . ." eh?

MICHAEL: But I would never want to say, "When in Nazi Germany, do as the Nazis do."

ELIZABETH: So you think some things are relative, but not everything. Could we get more clear about where you want to draw the line?

MICHAEL: Well, I think the line has to be drawn where we start to talk about right and wrong—morally, I mean. Or about what a good human being is like. You can certainly be a good human being and drive on the left-hand side of the road; but you can't be a good human being and send Jews to die in concentration camps.

FRED: Of course *we here in this room* would all agree with you. But we need to go deeper. *Why* would we all agree with you? Because we were brought up in America and not in Nazi Germany, that's why! If we had been raised *there,* our standards of what a good human being is like would have been different.

ELIZABETH: Before we start on that issue, do we agree that there are many things which people can just cheerfully differ about—the length of a man's hair, for instance, or what sorts of clothing are appropriate? We could say that custom is properly king over things like that.

MICHAEL: The fact that custom is king over certain things doesn't mean people will differ *cheerfully* about them. Do you remember that motorcycle trip I took after the summer of our sophomore year—with my long hair and beard? In more than one small town I thought I was going to get stomped.

ANITA: You can't say you weren't warned.

FRED: Looking at you now, I have a hard time believing you are the same person!

MICHAEL: I needed a job.

SAM: Mike's example raises a good question, though. *Can* we draw a line between what we can leave to custom and other things about which we wouldn't want to say that custom is king?

ELIZABETH: It seems to me that if relativism has any bite, it must be in connection with *what a good human life is like.* The question is whether custom is the deciding factor in *that* realm.

ANITA: I think we can accept that, but it's not going to be a perfectly clear separation. There are bound to be borderline disputes about whether something is or is not a moral issue. In some Moslem countries, for instance, women have to veil their faces in public. Is that "merely" a custom? Or is it a form of oppression with moral significance?

SAM: Still, there are clear cases. No one would think there's a moral question about which side of the road to drive on—as long as everyone in a community conforms. So I think we should agree. What we are talking about is whether custom is king over the issue of what makes for a good human being, or a good life.

PETER: Let me raise another issue here. I don't think that relativism bears only on questions of how to live, what you have called moral matters. I think it also bears on what to *believe*—what people think the world is like, for instance, the nature of human beings, and whether there is a God or gods. Cultures differ on these questions just as deeply as on the moral ones.

ELIZABETH: I think you are right, Peter. But we can't talk about everything at once. If you don't mind, let's set that aside as a topic for tomorrow evening.

PETER: Just so we don't forget to come back to it.

ELIZABETH: It's a promise. But right now we should get back to Fred's claim that if we lived in a different culture—Nazi Germany, for instance—we'd have different standards for a good human life. Do you have an argument for that view, Fred?

FRED: Nothing easier. Where do we get our values from, our sense of good and bad? From our parents, mostly; secondarily from teachers, schoolmates, friends, some of us from church; and from the stories we're told in the books our culture preserves and the television programs and movies we watch. Children just internalize the values of their society. We did it; that's how we turned out to be the people we are. Children in every society do it. And if we had been raised in a culture with very different values, then those are the values we would have.

SAM: You're forgetting about conscience. We all have that little voice inside that tells us when we are about to do something wrong. It's what kept Socrates from doing wrong, even though several times it put his life in danger and eventually led him to consent to his death. Some of us think of it as the voice of God.

FRED: Come on, Sam. You read *Huckleberry Finn*. Don't you remember the pangs of "conscience" Huck had every time he thought about helping Jim to escape from slavery? Again and again he simply couldn't bring himself to do it, "knowing" it was "wrong." And when he finally did it he thought he had consigned himself to hell for sure. Conscience is as much a product of our upbringing as any other part of our moral life.

ELIZABETH: Well, Fred has certainly given us something to chew on. But let's not go too fast. If I've got you right, Fred, you're saying that if we had been brought up in the Hitler Youth Movement, we would have had the same deplorable values (as we think of them from our present perspective) as the Nazis. And we would probably think of the values we now have as weak and decadent.

But not everyone in Nazi Germany went along with the evil. Some held out, some fled, some rebelled, and there was even an attempt on Hitler's life, though it was unsuccessful.

FRED: But that's no argument against my thesis. All it shows is that Nazi Germany was not a totally unified culture—that there were other influences at work as well. Those who resisted the dominant forces had been influenced in other ways to accept other values.

MICHAEL: Suppose we grant Fred's point for a moment. What follows from it? Sam said early on that "thinking so doesn't make it so." I agree with that. Thinking that a certain thickness of tubing will be adequate for a racing bike certainly doesn't *make* it adequate. Any engineer has experienced enough failures of *that* sort to know that thinking something is right doesn't make it right.

SAM: And even Fred allowed that just because Peter *thinks* he can ride up all the hills on this tour, that's no guarantee he can actually *do* it.

ANITA: So you both want to say that even if Fred's hypothesis about the origin of our moral values is correct—and most of us would have been good little Nazis in 1940's Germany—that wouldn't mean that the values we would have then had were the *right* ones. Or the *best* ones. Having values of some sort is one thing. Having *good* values is another.

MICHAEL: That's right. We might have turned out to be perfectly despicable people. But the fact that we would then have thought our values of absolute loyalty to the Reich, to the Führer, and to the Aryan race were the best and highest values wouldn't have made us any less despicable. *More* so, I would say.

FRED: But look at what you're doing here. You're making a judgment on the kind of person you would have been in *those circumstances* from a position in *these circumstances* where you are another kind of person. I don't see how you can do that.

Suppose we take your principle seriously. If it doesn't follow from a Nazi's *thinking* that he is exemplifying the highest values that he *actually is* exemplifying good values, then it doesn't follow from *your* judgment on the Nazis that *you* are manifesting good values now. You think you are, of course, but so did the Nazis. It's all relative to how you were brought up.

PETER: I must say, I like that argument. What's sauce for the goose is sauce for the gander. If Sam and Mike want to hold that thinking so doesn't make it so, then they have to admit this applies to their own thinking as well.

FRED: Right. How do they know *their* values are the right ones? And if they don't know that, what right do they have to stand in judgment even on the Nazis? Who's to say which values are the best?

ELIZABETH: I think we are going too fast here. Again we need to keep several issues distinct. Whether we have a right to judge others given the "custom is king" view is one question. Whether custom is indeed king is a different question. We can discuss both of those.

But right now we are asking about the implications of supposing that people's values are a pretty strict function of the society they grow up in. Sam and Michael argue that it doesn't follow from the fact that someone holds a certain value that it is a good one. And Fred and Peter point out that if this is a good principle it has to apply to our own values as well. Could we all agree so far?

FRED: No, I don't agree. My argument was simply that Sam and Mike can't have it both ways. They can't, on the one hand, hold that *other people's values* may diverge from "the true good" and assume that *their own values* do not! But that's just what they seem to be doing when they call other ways of life "despicable."

I don't even admit the distinction they are relying on. As far as I can see, there's no sense in thinking you can discover which values are *really good* values, apart from the values people *actually hold*.

ANITA: Can you say a little more about that?

FRED: Sure. It's not a difficult point. To distinguish what is *really* good from what *seems* good to you (or to anyone else) you would have to jump out of your skin and look at things from some "objective" vantage point. I don't believe we can do that. We would need to measure what we deeply, sincerely, and truly think against some independent standard of goodness that we can clearly see, get our values lined up with it, and then be in a position to judge the values of others. I don't believe there is any such standard — or any such vantage point either.

SAM: Maybe you have just described the vantage point of God.

FRED: Well, I don't think we need to settle whether God exists to get on with the issue of relativism! Even if there were such a vantage point, it wouldn't be one any of *us* could occupy. So for us, it's as good as if it weren't there at all.

SAM: Unless, of course, God has told us, or maybe *shown* us, what the good human life is like.

FRED: This sounds like an argument we used to have ten years ago.

SAM: It's a possibility you couldn't rule out then, and I don't think you can do it now either.

FRED: But don't you see that your claim about God's "revelation"—I guess that's what you call it—is not an *escape* from the custom-is-king principle, but an *illustration* of it? That's just how you and those in your sub-culture see things; you think God reveals the truth to us, but others think no such thing.

SAM: But some ways of seeing things may be the *right* ways of seeing them.

FRED: And how can you tell whether your way is the right way unless you can jump out of your cultural skin and see things bare—uncontaminated by what custom makes "obvious" to you?

ANITA: *Déja vu* all over again, as Yogi Berra once said! I doubt whether this particular argument is going to get us anywhere. But we might ask about something Fred and Sam both seem to presuppose. They seem to think that we need to occupy some "objective" point of view to be justified in making moral assessments; they assume that unless we can get a sort of "view from nowhere"[2] we can't have any confidence in our judgments about the good life for human beings. They disagree in that Fred thinks there is no such point of view and Sam believes we have been granted access to it. But I want to resist that assumption altogether.

ELIZABETH: You want to say that even if we can't jump out of our skins, as Fred puts it, we needn't be forced into a custom-is-king sort of relativism.

ANITA: Exactly.

ELIZABETH: That's an important possibility. But to explore it I think we need to get clearer about just what this relativism is we are trying to discuss.

PETER: You are right about that. And it's easily done. I recall from philosophy class—yes, I do remember something I learned there—that one of the early Greek thinkers, Protagoras, said that *man is*

---

2. The quoted phrase is taken from the title of a book by Thomas Nagel, *The View From Nowhere* (Oxford University Press, 1986).

the measure of all things.[3] That means that things *are* as they *seem* to you to be.

FRED: It's a denial that there is any objective or absolute standard available for "measuring" or judging rightness and wrongness, good and evil. If something seems good to you, then it *is* good — for you. And if something (maybe even the same thing) seems bad to me, then it *is* bad — for me. And that's all there is to be said.

MICHAEL: Let's see if I have this straight. Protagoras says, and it sounds like you two agree, that there is nothing at all — or at least nothing we can tap into — that constrains or puts any limits on what I could *rightly* find evil or good? That it's all just a matter of *opinion?*

FRED: That's what I think.

SAM: There is no way I can accept *that*. And I don't think any of the rest of you could really, sincerely accept it either. Suppose I have a child in my dentist's chair. And suppose I find there is nothing wrong with her teeth. But I take out my drill and drill deep into a sound tooth without giving any anesthetic because I enjoy hearing the screams of children. Now *that's* evil. And if I did it, *I* would be an evil person. And I'm willing to stand here and affirm that this isn't "just my opinion," or "just how it seems to me."

FRED: A pretty extreme example, Sam.

SAM: But just right to make the point. I bet even you would think this deed horribly, indescribably, *absolutely* evil. Tell me now, could you sit in that office and just *watch*, saying, "Well, in my opinion he shouldn't do that, but if it seems good to Sam . . ."

FRED: What if I were to do just that?

SAM: Then *you* would be an evil person, too. But you couldn't do it, could you?

3. Protagoras says, "Of all things the measure is man: of existing things, that they exist; of non-existing things, that they do not exist." (John Manley Robinson, *An Introduction to Early Greek Philosophy* [Houghton Mifflin Co., 1968], p. 245).

FRED: No, of course not. But that's not fair.

MICHAEL: It seems fair enough. You were arguing that unless we could occupy an objective point of view we would have no right to judge others—and that there is no such point of view. According to you, all we have are opinions. It seems to follow that we can't make moral judgments about others. But if you can't even make a judgment, how could you justify interfering with Sam's horrible work? You have your opinion; Sam has his. What seems bad *to you* seems good *to him*. What more can you say?

ANITA: But you can't bring yourself to be consistent here. You *would* interfere. And I think we would all applaud your character while deploring your principles.

PETER: Let me help Fred out here. Of course he would interfere; so, I hope, would we all. But that wouldn't be inconsistent unless we assume that we can't judge another's good or evil character without an impossible God-like objectivity. Maybe a relativist doesn't need to be married to that principle. I agree with Fred that we have no "external" point of view from which to judge. But do we need it in order to make judgments?

Why couldn't a relativist say something like this: "Although it seems good to Sam to do this useless and very painful drilling, it seems bad to me. Since I judge it is a bad thing to do, I should interfere even though I know that Sam disagrees"? There's nothing incoherent about that.

ANITA: I agree we don't need an external view. And there is nothing incoherent in what you say. But it seems a strange thing for a *relativist* to hold. I thought the main merit of relativism was its claim to overcome ethnocentrism—our inclination to think *our* ways are best. But now you seem to be saying that acting on our ethnocentric views is OK. In this case, you are suggesting that a relativist could judge, and even interfere, simply on the basis that this is what seems best to him.

MICHAEL: Yes, what's happened to the relativism?

PETER: Look, I'm just trying to point out that relativists needn't be immobilized by their convictions. In a situation like this a relativist could always pick up the phone and call the police. If they were told what is about to happen, they would be right over.

ELIZABETH: That's just passing the buck, Peter. And it won't work, anyway. Why call the police rather than a television studio? Some choice footage available there!

ANITA: Let's try to think carefully here. We've got to imagine that Fred has *two* thoughts in his mind. One amounts to the judgment that Sam is about to do a very bad thing. The other is a thought *about* this first thought, namely that this judgment of his is only an opinion, no more warranted in the final analysis than any other. In particular, Fred thinks (in this second thought): "My judgment that Sam is doing a terrible thing is no more absolutely or objectively correct than Sam's opinion that drilling the un-anaesthetized tooth would be an interesting way to spend ten minutes." Or, to put it another way, the second thought is: "Sam's opinion is as good as mine."

Now, here's my question: doesn't this second thought *undermine* the first one? If you hold the second thought vividly in mind, it seems to make the first one perfectly arbitrary, doesn't it? If you, Fred, were fully conscious of everything you believe, wouldn't you suffer a kind of *paralysis*? If you avoided every kind of self-deception, wouldn't you see that you have *no reason* to interfere with Sam's nasty practices? And if you have no reason to act, then why couldn't you just as reasonably sit there passively and watch?

ELIZABETH: This is a very important issue. I think people *are* sometimes reduced to apathy by their relativistic convictions. They think all value judgments are equal in validity, so they refrain from making them—and from acting on them. So they think they can't interfere if children are abused in a certain culture, or if wives are beaten or young girls are ritually mutilated. After all, they think, their values may be as good as ours.

ANITA: Horrible!

FRED: But in this case I *would* have the thought that it is a bad thing to drill into that tooth. Why couldn't I just act on that? It is an opinion of mine, after all.

ANITA: The question is what happens to that opinion when it is joined to the second opinion—that the first is *just* an opinion and no more legitimate than its opposite. Can it still produce behavior?

MICHAEL: Fred, I think you are in even worse shape than Anita argued. You are the one, after all, who argued earlier that all our views are just the product of our conditioning. You would have to keep that thought in mind, too. And that would make you think that if you had been brought up like Sam, you'd enjoy hurting people too. Once you realize that both your moral judgment and Sam's "perverse" enjoyments are merely products of your environments, how could you reasonably prefer to act on one rather than on another? They just seem like two ways nature operates. Impersonal nature produced you with your values and Sam with his. From that point of view, your earlier question is quite in order: Who's to say which is better?

SAM: Let's remember, please, that it's not *me* we're talking about here, but a *fictional* Sam! Purely hypothetical, that's all.

MICHAEL: Right, Sam. If you were the sort of person who could really do that kind of thing, I don't think any of us would want to be on this tour with you. But my point is that relativists are in a tough spot. On the one hand they have their opinions, including judgments about good and evil; on the other hand they have "second-order" opinions, opinions that all of these first-order judgments are unjustified, none of them closer to the truth of the matter than any other (since there is no truth of the matter, and opinions are merely the products of blind environmental conditioning). And, as Anita and Liz say, these second opinions will tend to undermine the first.

FRED: Well, I don't know. Every animal acts on the basis of how things seem to it: it seems good to the fox to stalk the rabbit and it seems good to the rabbit to flee the fox. If I don't like what Sam is up to, I don't see why I can't try to put a stop to it.

ANITA: The point is that you aren't like other animals; they don't have thoughts about the status of their likes and dislikes, but humans do. And in order to act well, these thoughts and desires need to be in harmony. The argument here has been that the relativist will have a hard time getting a kind of equilibrium in his thoughts, that some of them will tend to undercut the power of others to move us to action.

FRED: Well, I'm sorry, but that just sounds far-fetched to me. The moment I hear the first scream from that poor girl, I'm going to knock Sam flat on his rear. Harmony of thoughts and equilibrium be damned!

ELIZABETH: That may be right, in a way. Relativistic thoughts may often be too "weak" to disarm action in a real situation. But there does nevertheless seem to be a kind of incoherence in the relativist's view. It's as though relativists have to *forget* some of their convictions in order to act with any decisiveness.

And it does look to me as though relativism has a *tendency* to undermine action.

PETER: I still don't see paralysis as a real threat to the relativist. It's true that someone who thinks no opinion is more *objectively* justified than its opposite has no *objective* reason for acting against the opposite opinion. But such a person will also think no opinion is any *less* (objectively) justified than any other.

There are two thoughts here. First, it's not as though Fred suspects Sam may be *right*; there's no right and wrong about it, from an objective point of view. So, since Fred does think Sam shouldn't drill into that tooth, why shouldn't he act on his thought? Second, Fred may have *his own* reasons for interfering, even if they can't be objectively validated.

ANITA: Very interesting. Suppose we spin Peter's thought out a bit. Peter wants to say, in effect, that the *entire* second-order thought of a relativist is that, objectively speaking, first-order opinions are *neither* justified *nor* unjustified; and so there is no incoherence in a relativist's taking action on his first-order views. The justification question, as it were, cancels itself out.

But there may be a new worry here. I wonder whether Fred's reaction is not a telling one. He said he would knock Sam on his butt. If we give up on the matter of justifying our views, of trying to give *reasons* for our actions, aren't we left with nothing but a power struggle?

FRED: If you think life is anything *but* a power struggle, you are pretty naive, Anita.

PETER: Don't go too fast here. Before it gets to the point of a fight, there is a lot they could do. They could talk. Fred could try to persuade Sam to see things his way. And he might succeed. Remember that Protagoras and the other sophists all taught rhetoric—the art of persuasive speaking. They thought this was the way to resolve differences, not by violence.

ELIZABETH: That's an important point. The interesting question, however, is whether rhetoric can be anything but an exercise of power by means other than physical violence. But let's leave that for tomorrow night. For now, perhaps we could agree that while Sam's example puts a kind of pressure on the relativist, it doesn't by itself disqualify the view as inconsistent.

MICHAEL: It's worth noting, though, that Fred has changed his mind about an important topic. He started out arguing that without an objective standpoint from which to judge between divergent opinions, we couldn't judge; and that meant we couldn't have a basis on which we could interfere. But now he and Peter are both saying that the lack of a "view from nowhere" is no barrier to interference. Which way does he want it?

FRED: Maybe what I should say is that without an objective point of view we don't have a right to judge or interfere in the sense that *rights just don't come into it*. They could come into it only from a point of view we can't have. The situation is this: We just *will* interfere where we feel strongly. Furthermore, without an objective viewpoint we can't say there are any *duties* either. So I don't have any duty *not* to interfere. So again, why shouldn't I?

ANITA: Well, that's a clear enough position, if rather unattractive.

FRED: Unattractive by *your* lights, you mean.

ANITA: But I'd like to pursue the inconsistency issue in a somewhat different direction. Fred says that the relativist (speaking for himself here, and maybe for Peter, too) . . .

PETER: I'll speak for myself, thank you.

ANITA: . . . that the relativist denies any objective or absolute standard for judging opinions. So all we have are opinions. But then this is just an opinion, too, isn't it—that all we have are opinions? Just one opinion among others? Suppose, contrary to Fred, someone has the opinion that there *is* an absolute standard. On the relativist's own principles, this opinion is just as good as the opinion that there *isn't* any absolute standard.

MICHAEL: You mean that from a relativist's own point of view the opinion that relativism is false must be as acceptable as the opinion that it is true. Oh, that's good! I really like that.

ELIZABETH: I think there is also another way to make Anita's point. The relativist's denial of an objective point of view seems to be made from just such a point of view. Fred wants to say, *"There is no such point of view!"* But from what point of view is this being said? He seems pretty definite about it.

ANITA: Yes. It seems that the relativist's point must be expressed in such a way as to undercut the very point it makes. Just as much as the absolutist, the relativist seems to presuppose a kind of objectivity in making his claim.

FRED: Wait a minute. I didn't mean to say that relativism is *true.* Or at least not *TRUE* in some absolute sense. All I wanted to say is that it is true *for me.* So you can't zap me with a contradiction here. I can allow that while it may be true for me, you may not agree; it may not be true for you.

ELIZABETH: What in the world does "true for me" mean?

FRED: It means, "That's how I see it."

ANITA: Fred, it does seem like you face a dilemma. Either you deny absolute standards absolutely—and then you do seem to be caught in a contradiction. Or else your denial has no force for anyone else. It makes no claim that anyone else needs to consider and expresses a purely private impression on your part: how it seems to you.

MICHAEL: Taken the first way relativism pretty clearly refutes itself. It tries to occupy the objective point of view in the very act of claiming no such point of view exists.

SAM: And taken the second way it doesn't seem any better—on its own principles!—than anti-relativism. You have your opinion and I have mine. Relativism may be true for you, but it isn't true for me! Ha![4]

ANITA: So what do you say to this argument, Fred?

FRED: Hmmm.

PETER: I was afraid Fred would get himself backed into this corner; that's why I said I wanted to speak for myself. To assert relativism the way he wanted to is bound to lead to trouble. It's like the skeptic who says, "Nothing can be known." There is an old and easy rejoinder to that claim. You ask the skeptic, "How do you know that?" So it looks like the skeptic undercuts himself in stating the skeptical thesis—claiming to know something in the act of disclaiming knowledge. But the smart skeptic won't get caught that way, and the smart relativist won't either.

FRED: I don't understand.

PETER: You got into trouble because you wanted to make relativism into a kind of theory—a *doctrine* which could be stated and defended. And then it looked like it either had to be an objective doctrine or a purely private opinion. We could call the relativism Fred was defending *dogmatic relativism,* since it asserts the relativistic thesis as a belief or dogma.

But I think we should learn from the old skeptics. They didn't *assert* that nothing could be known. That way, they clearly saw, lay only trouble. Rather, when someone claimed to know something about reality they would assemble reasons to shake their opponent's confidence in it.

4. Alan Garfinkel has been quoted as saying to his California students, "You may not be coming from where I am coming from, but I know relativism isn't *true for me*" (Hilary Putnam, *Reason, Truth and History* [Cambridge, 1981], p. 119).

MICHAEL: And you think you can do something parallel for the relativist, do you? You think that there is a way of being a relativist which escapes Anita's inconsistency objection?

PETER: As a matter of fact, yes.

MICHAEL: I think we'd all like to hear that!

PETER: Well, this by itself won't convince you, but a good place to start might be to think about the harm that so-called "good" people do. I mean people who claim to be connected by a hot line to goodness and truth. I doubt that the agony wreaked on the world in the course of history by skeptics and relativists has been more than a thousandth of that perpetrated by those dogmatists who were convinced of their objectivity and the absolute truth of their beliefs.

Think of colonialism, the "white man's burden," the forced conversions, the massacres failing conversion, the destruction of native ways of life that had sufficed for countless generations and their replacement with foreign ways that were empty shells, the new diseases, the over-population with consequent starvation. Or think of the religious wars that are still suffusing parts of the globe with suffering, wars fought by people who are fanatically convinced they have it "right." All these "benefits" are conferred by those confident they have the right to judge others and interfere because they have the TRUTH.

ANITA: We are all aware of the horrors of history, Peter. But I have a question. You talk of the "harm" done. Why aren't you in exactly the same dilemma Fred was in? Do you mean harm in some objectively certifiable sense, or is it just your opinion that this is harm?

PETER: Neither. I am inviting you to mean by "harm" whatever you ordinarily mean by the word. I am playing your game, if you like. And I am asking you whether in that sense of harm *you* don't have to admit that an awful lot of it has been done by *objectivists* and *absolutists* about values.

SAM: I don't get it. Are you claiming that these folks have done harm or not?

PETER: Think of it this way. For the time being, I am playing a game according to your rules. It's not the game I usually play, but I can play your game, too. Imagine a baseball player taking up cricket; he plays according to the rules of cricket. So I'm not making any assertion at all about harm, just asking questions, which you can answer in your own terms.

MICHAEL: OK, I understand that, I think. But what's the point?

PETER: I'm just trying to shake you up a bit. Most of you seem so confident that there is some objective and absolute good and evil—*and* that you know what it is. It might give you pause to acknowledge how much evil, *according to your own standards*, has been done by people with just those convictions.

ELIZABETH: I think we have to acknowledge that in our sense of harm, people who are "good" in the sense you describe have done a lot of harm.

PETER: Thank you. Maybe a little more of that "tendency to undermine action" Liz was talking about would be a good thing.

ELIZABETH: But I have a question, too. And an answer to it may give you less to be proud of than you think. Even if we admit that absolutists have done harm, why should we admit that they did these evils *because* they were absolutists? Perhaps it isn't the conviction that there is an absolute goodness which is to blame, but something else.

PETER: For instance?

ELIZABETH: It might be overconfidence in *their having got it right* about the absolute good. You can believe in the absoluteness of goodness without identifying it with what you yourself believe. You can even believe in the universality of moral rules without feeling certain that the rules *you* accept are fit to be universalized.
  So the evil done might be due to a failure in self-criticism.

SAM: Saints, in fact—those we think closest to some sort of absolute goodness—are usually those who are most conscious of how far they still are from achieving it.

ELIZABETH: Or the profession of belief in absolute values by the people you are calling "good" may just be a rationalization; they will do whatever they will do, but it's nice for them to be able to think they are doing it for God or country or the benefit of the natives who are being slaughtered. I think a lot of the more deplorable actions of European adventurers in the New World can be accounted for in this way. If Christianity hadn't been around to supply a convenient rationalization, they would have seized on something else.

MICHAEL: I think Liz is pointing out that we don't have to agree that Peter's "good" people are really *good*. I myself don't think they are.

PETER: Liz makes some good points. Still, there seems to be a fairly strong connection between dogmatism about the good and insensitivity to alternative ways of life.

ELIZABETH: Perhaps that's so. But let me put my point in those terms: How strong is the connection between my believing in the reality of absolute good and evil and my being dogmatic about my convictions—my being certain *I* am right? *That's* the connection that needs to be made if we are to be shaken to the core—if we are to give up believing in absolute goodness and retreat to relativism. You need to show us that relativism is the *only* alternative to insensitive dogmatism. You haven't done that.

ANITA: There is also another issue here. Do relativists do no harm—in our sense of harm? You recall that line from Dostoyevsky's *The Brothers Karamazov*: "If God is dead, then everything is permitted." Smerdyakov murders the old Karamazov father on just those grounds—relativist grounds, as they seem to me.

ELIZABETH: Perhaps humans are so perverse they will do terrible things no matter what their convictions about absolute value.

MICHAEL: Maybe we should agree that you can't refute a view on the grounds that someone might abuse it. Absolutists have done terrible things, and so have relativists. The question, as Liz put it earlier, is whether they have done these things *because* of their absolutism or relativism—or for other reasons.

ANITA: That's a hard question about motivation. And at the moment I don't think the answer is clear.

PETER: All right, all right. All I wanted to do for now was to undermine any confidence there might be that believing in absolute truth and goodness might guarantee—even in your own terms—heaven on earth.

ANITA: I guess you can consider that done. But what's next?

ELIZABETH: It's getting late and the itinerary calls for a long ride tomorrow. I think the next thing should be bed.

FRED: What a good idea! My brain has been half shut down for the last twenty minutes.

SAM: We noticed that; but we thought it had been longer.

ELIZABETH: Let's start tomorrow evening with Peter telling us more about his version of relativism—the one that promises to escape the self-refutations we discovered tonight. That should lead us nicely into the issue he posed earlier, too, about a relativism of belief as well as of value. And the question of persuasion and power may find a natural home in that discussion as well.

MICHAEL: Peter, you had better gather your strength for the hills to come!

PETER: Worry about your own strength, Mike. I'm determined not to walk.

ANITA: I'm looking forward to the ride *and* the conversation. Goodnight all.

The Second Conversation

The Evening of Their Third Day Together

SAM: What great dinners these country inns serve!

MICHAEL: After today's energy drain, a good stoking-up is what I needed.

PETER: I must say, this afternoon I used up about all the energy I had.

ANITA: But you didn't walk?

PETER: No, I didn't walk.

ELIZABETH: Perhaps you are too tired, though, to continue our conversation of last night?

PETER: No. My body may not be in the best shape, but the brain's not tired. It could use some exercise. I'd enjoy some more discussion.

ANITA: So would I. As I remember, Peter was going to begin tonight by telling us more about that "non-dogmatic" form of relativism he thinks he can defend.

FRED: Before he does that, can I make some amendments to the views I was getting pounded for yesterday? As I was grinding up a couple of those monster hills, I thought I saw a way out of the difficulties you were forcing on me.

PETER: It's OK with me if you want to begin. Give me a little longer to enjoy the coffee.

FRED: Well, it came to me that the relativism I was defending is too individualistic. I sort of slid into saying that since there is no accessible source of absolute goodness to judge by, the good was what seemed good to each person. But now I think that was a mistake. There *is* a standard for measuring good and evil, but it isn't the individual's opinion. It is the rules and practices, the customs, of a culture. That was what Herodotus was saying, after all. It's not the individual who is king, but *custom*.

MICHAEL: You mean that a good human life is defined or specified by a group rather than an individual—by the group to which an individual belongs.

FRED: Yes, but not in a book of rules or definitions. It is specified by the way they bring up children, by what the adults (or the respected adults) praise and blame, by the examples they set in their own behavior, by what they are proud of and what they feel ashamed of.

ANITA: Would you say that the *law* is an important part of specifying the good for a culture?

FRED: Yes, of course. But the relevant customs can't be restricted to the law; law tends to govern external behavior—and not even all of that which is important to us. In any case, I now want to say that there *are* duties and obligations—and rights, too. And these are specified in the practices of a culture.

I now think I have a better account of why I should try to stop Sam from doing his dastardly deed. It *is* wrong to inflict pain on an innocent child just for your own enjoyment. And if Sam, or anyone, were to do something like that, he *would* be a wicked, evil person—and should be stopped. And the reason is that in our culture, such cruelty is simply not tolerated.

ANITA: According to this view, then, there really are good and evil deeds. But they are not *absolutely* good and evil; Sam's (fictional) cruelty, for example, is evil *relative to the standards of our culture*.

FRED: That's what I should have been maintaining all along yesterday.

ELIZABETH: We could call this *cultural relativism* perhaps, in contrast with the *individualist relativism* you were defending last night.

FRED: That sounds like a good name for it.

ANITA: Well, it may be an improvement on your earlier views, but I have some questions.

FRED: I might have known you would have. Lawyers always do.

ANITA: The first question concerns the notion of a culture. If you want to say that morality is relative to a culture, don't you need to say what a culture is? Otherwise, how can you tell when you have one culture and when there are two? There may be simple cases, but mostly it doesn't seem to me to be so easy. We each belong to a lot of groups, associations, families, religions, parties, a nation. Which of them counts as a culture? All? Some?

MICHAEL: I think that's a problem all right. It's true that they all have some influence on us. And they don't all agree in their values, either. If you want to say that people are to be judged by the values of their culture, don't you have to be able to pick out just what "their culture" is? I don't see how you are going to do that.

ANITA: And even when you can, it is likely, in our modern world especially, that people will belong to more than one culture. Take me, for example. I'm a product of Spanish-American culture, but also of that rarefied culture instilled by a law school. And I consider myself a feminist. I suppose you could call all of these "cultures" of a sort.

So here's the second question: If people belong to several cultures, which is the relevant one to judge by?

ELIZABETH: That is not an idle question. Think of the court cases over the responsibility of Christian Scientist parents for their children's health. These people are both citizens of our country and members of a church with unusual views about sickness and healing. Should they be judged according to the dictates of their religion or according to standards of normal American health care?

ANITA: And there are other cases like that in the law, too: Whether Amish children should be forced to go to public school, whether native Americans can use peyote in religious rituals, and so on. All these are clashes between cultural values for people who are members of several cultures.

MICHAEL: The upshot, Fred, is that though it may sound clear enough to say that good and evil are relative to a culture, it's not going to be much help in practice, unless you can say in each case what a culture is and which one is the relevant one.

FRED: Still, I think all the cultures both Sam and I belong to would condemn "Sam's dastardly deed." So at least in cases like this (where there is either just one culture or the several cultures agree) I think it works. Wanton cruelty is wrong because it is judged to be wrong by our culture – or cultures.

ANITA: That brings me to my third question. Your present view seems to allow for judgments within a culture, intra-cultural judgments, we might call them. Your condemnation of Sam's cruelty would be an example. But what about judgments across cultures? Do I have to judge the Nazi according to the standards of *his* culture? If so, how can I condemn the holocaust?

SAM: If you can't condemn the holocaust on your principles, then there is something very wrong with your principles!

MICHAEL: In a way, it's even worse than that. Suppose we allow that Nazi culture is one thing and Jewish culture a different thing. If we have to judge by the standards of the relevant culture, then it looks like from the Nazi point of view we have to *praise* the "final solution," but from the Jewish point of view it must be *condemned* as an indescribable evil. So we will end up praising and condemning the very same thing!

ANITA: And finally, I wonder whether cultural relativism doesn't have the same problems that we discovered last night in the individualistic kind. Fred wants to say that good and evil are relative to a culture. But don't we have to ask, "From what point of view is this being asserted?" Presumably Fred doesn't think he can say it from some neutral, objective point of view, so it must be said from within a certain culture.

FRED: I see where you are going. You are going to say that if the assertion of cultural relativism is made from within a culture, then a relativist has to agree that the claim of relativism is itself valid only relative to that culture.

MICHAEL: And someone who isn't part of that culture could assert the opposite – with just as much right.

FRED: And then I would have to say that the *denial* of cultural relativism is just as true for that person as its *assertion* is for me.

MICHAEL: And if, to escape that unhappy outcome, you do say that it is objectively true that standards are culture-relative, then you are relying on a non-relative standard to deny there are any non-relative standards.

FRED: Well, I don't know. I guess I give up. But I *still* think there is something right about relativism.

PETER: So do I. And I think we've been too hard on Fred. If we take a more charitable attitude, I think we can see that there is something valuable that Fred is trying to protect. He wants to avoid what we called *ethnocentrism*, the view that we in our culture know it all and have got it right about the best life for humans to live. So he is trying to find a way to avoid the pride and arrogance, the smug self-satisfaction and contempt – and perhaps that condescending "tolerance" – that so often permeates encounters with alien ways of living and doing things. And I think that is a very worthwhile motivation.

FRED: Thanks Pete. That's the first kind thing anyone has had to say about my views so far.

PETER: Your heart's in the right place, and I think we need to acknowledge that. Your problem is that you can't resist trying to formulate your relativism as a kind of doctrine. Your cultural relativism is just as *dogmatic* as the individualist version. As we saw last night, and again just now, that always gets you into trouble.

ELIZABETH: Well, that is about as good an introduction as you could want to a presentation of your own views, Peter. Let's hear what you have to say.

PETER: In a way I don't really have a "view" or a "position." It's more like a denial that a view or position can be established. Or rather, since even that sounds like a *thesis*, it's that I think I can show anyone who does have a view on these matters that they don't have any good reason for accepting that view. To put it another way, I think I can show you that there are equally good reasons for competing views.

SAM: That sounds awfully negative to me.

PETER: So it may. But I don't mean it to be just destructive or despairing; I mean it to be a humane and liberating thing. Perhaps I should set the stage by saying something about the motivations for it.

SAM: Please do.

PETER: I think people are often too quick to leap to judgments about things beyond their experience. They dismiss what they don't understand – strange treatments for the ill, different moral codes, other religions – alien ways of thinking and behaving. Or they interpret what they see in terms of familiar patterns that don't fit at all. These misunderstandings can sometimes be funny; they are exploited in jokes and humorous stories. But fundamentally I think they are sad because they separate people from each other and degrade opportunities for the enrichment of life into just more of the same. In extreme cases they cause prejudicial treatment, quarrels and wars.

MICHAEL: This is familiar enough. What's the point?

PETER: The point is coming. But first let me recall that old saying, "Nothing human is alien to me." That's the ideal behind my form of relativism. I think we can benefit from an acquaintance with—no, from a *sympathetic identification* with the extremely different ways of life humans have developed. Christians can profit from understanding Buddhist practices and atheists from native American spirituality. Modern medicine should not be too quick to dismiss folk remedies and even our prestigious science must not assume it is the key to understanding reality.

What I want is a kind of *openness* to the variety of ways in which people have interpreted the world. Or, as I might almost say, I want a recognition of the many different *worlds* in which people actually live. I might add that I think literature is about the best way to gain such understanding.

SAM: That sounds open-minded and noble enough. I wonder, though, whether open-mindedness can't be taken too far—leaving you empty-headed.

But, as Mike asked earlier, what's the point?

PETER: I think we are ready for that now. If you explore, with charity and sympathy, a view radically different from your own, I think you find there are no good reasons to prefer your own view to that one—or that one to yours.

SAM: Wait a minute. What about something like anti-semitism? Do you think it's as legitimate a view as one of mutual respect among persons?

PETER: I detest anti-semitism and racism as much as you do, Sam. But I think if we are honest with ourselves, we have to admit we don't have any *objectively convincing reason* to do so.

MICHAEL: A moment ago you were saying that nothing human is alien to you; and now you say you detest racism. Being a racist is certainly a "human" thing. Do I detect a contradiction here?

PETER: Not at all. I don't have to *approve* of everything I have charitably tried to understand in others—any more than I have to endorse all the whims and urges that *I* sometimes feel—and yet they are human too (all too human, some might say). In fact, I *couldn't* approve them all, without succumbing to absolute confusion or the empty-headedness Sam is worried about. My point

about openness was directed against premature or offhand judging, judging *before* the serious attempt to understand. That's what
I think happens all too often.

MICHAEL: But you also want to say that we have no *reason* to prefer
one view to another. How far do you want to push this claim? You
don't mean, do you, that some "primitive" animistic notions
about spirits in the trees and gods causing storms are as reasonable as scientific accounts of these matters?

PETER: Strange as it may seem, Mike, that's exactly what I do
mean.

ELIZABETH: If I'm not mistaken, we are now opening up that
broader question Peter urged us to consider yesterday: whether
some sort of relativism applies to our beliefs about the world, and
not just to issues about the good life.

ANITA: I was hoping we would come to this. The moral issues are
important, of course, but I have the feeling that they can't be
separated from issues of belief generally, whether scientific, com-
monsensical, religious, or what have you. And I guess Peter
agrees.

PETER: I do indeed.

ANITA: But you seem to have quite astonishing views about these
beliefs. I think you owe us some explanation.

PETER: Since I don't have any relativistic doctrine to expound or
beliefs to defend, maybe the best way to explain is by examining
some of the differences we have right here in our group. Sam, you
are a believer, aren't you? You believe in God?

SAM: You all know I do.

PETER: Could you tell us why?

SAM: Well, there are lots of reasons. For one thing, I don't think
this marvelous world—all this beauty we are riding through every

day—happened just by accident; but I don't think I can *prove* that. Then there is the fact that most people of every age and place have had a sense of the sacred, have believed in God or the gods; so there is a kind of near-universal testimony of mankind in its favor. But I know that some people think this is an illusion of some kind.

So I guess I have to say that the main reason I actually believe in God is that I trust the people who report their experience of God's influence in their lives. They seem to be good people, not mixed up or crazy, sometimes saints. And I think you find the most convincing record of that influence in the Bible. And finally, most conclusively I suppose, my own experience fits what they have to say.

PETER: And, Michael, you are, I believe, an atheist or an agnostic?

MICHAEL: I don't know whether or not there is a God like the one Sam believes in; so I guess I'd describe myself as an agnostic.

FRED: I'm the atheist in the bunch.

SAM: The most *you* are entitled to say is that God doesn't exist *for you*. I don't find that very interesting!

PETER: I think Fred has been the target long enough. Let me concentrate on Sam and Mike. If I can do my thing on them, it should be pretty obvious how to extend it to the atheist. Mike, why do you think it's better to be an agnostic than a believer?

MICHAEL: Well, I think it is best to stick to what our senses can tell us about reality. And the best account we've got on that basis is the story science tells us.

PETER: Do you think, Mike, you could convince Sam to restrict his beliefs to the beliefs science can warrant?

MICHAEL: I haven't so far.

PETER: And Sam, do you think you could bring Mike over to your side?

SAM: I haven't so far.

PETER: But you've talked about it?

SAM: Sure. Quite a lot.

PETER: Why do you think he is so hard to persuade?

SAM: Well, he's got this idea that you have to be objective about things, scientific. As he just said, he wants to restrict what we believe to what can be tested by sense experience.

PETER: Why do you think we should do that, Michael?

MICHAEL: Because that's something people can all agree about. Anyone can read a ruler or an instrument dial; and with training we can all see what's to be seen through a microscope. We can all add and subtract and, again with the proper training, solve differential equations.

There's a kind of objectivity here. It's not a matter of subjective opinion what the thermometer reads. Once you leave this firm ground, anything goes—astrological predictions, claims about remembered earlier lives, gods and angels and spirits of wildly different and uncountable sorts. And there is no way to test any of that stuff. It's all contaminated with subjective factors: dreams, wishful thinking, fears, hopes. . . .

SAM: That's just not so. There *are* ways of testing claims about the supernatural. The church has been sorting out valid beliefs from heretical ones from the very start. The creeds are a result of this sorting. And the final test is always this: Is it in conformity with scripture?

MICHAEL: But don't you see how parochial that is, how subjective? Here I have to agree with Fred. You say we should test our beliefs by the Bible. But why not test them by the Koran? Or the Book of Mormon? Millions of people do, you know.

SAM: Those may all have some value. I don't want to deny that other religions have some part of the truth. But looked at from the viewpoint of scripture, they can be seen to have only part of the truth, and much error as well.

MICHAEL: And what if you looked at Christianity from the point of view of the Koran? Wouldn't you come to the same conclusion, but now in favor of Islam? That's why I think we should be hard-headed and stick to what we can all agree is reliable – the testimony of the senses, together with logic and mathematics. For the rest, let's confess that we just don't know.

PETER: I find this sort of exchange most interesting. What seems to be coming out is that the disagreement between Sam and Michael is a difference in *standards* for belief. Sam appeals to what he considers an authoritative source – and so does Mike. But they choose different authorities. Mike wants to rely on "the testimony of the senses," as he calls it, while Sam relies on the testimony of certain individuals who have left us a record of their religious experiences.

ELIZABETH: But isn't this just the sort of disagreement that *philosophy* is supposed to settle? I thought that what philosophers call "theory of knowledge" was supposed to set standards for what we can know, to give us rules for separating out what is legitimate knowledge from what only pretends to be.

PETER: So it was. And for several hundred years philosophers have pinned their hopes on *epistemology*, to give it its fancy name. But so far as I can see, all this effort by all these really smart people has come to nothing. Descartes thought we would be all right if we just stick to clear and distinct ideas; but that has proved hopeless, and everyone admits it. Either what is agreed to as clear and distinct is so minimal and empty you can't go on from there, or there is no agreement.

More promisingly, the empiricists thought we could build the edifice of knowledge on sense experience – just as Mike is still recommending. But if I am not mistaken, it is widely agreed that this won't work either.

MICHAEL: Why not? It seems sensible to me.

PETER: Because there is too much "play" in the theories that are supposed to be built on the senses. Think about your phrase, "the testimony of the senses." In fact, the senses don't "testify" to anything at all. They just register colors, shapes, sounds, tastes, and so on. These facts are just facts — like any other facts in nature. They don't themselves tell us what they *mean*. What science does (and common sense too, for that matter) is to *interpret* what the senses offer. And all such interpretations or theories, as they are called in the sciences, involve elements that go far beyond what the senses could tell us — if they could say anything at all! This is something even a non-relativist has to admit.

ANITA: Well, sure. I admit it, and I think Mike should too. But how are you going to get from there to the outrageous view that there is just as much reason to believe one thing as another? That's an awfully big leap.

MICHAEL: Maybe you could persuade us to make the leap if you tell us why explaining storms in terms of gods or spirits is as good as explaining them in terms of temperature, air pressure, winds, humidity, and so on.

PETER: Well, it wouldn't be as good for us. That sort of explanation wouldn't fit with the rest of our way of life. And it is perfectly understandable if you think it absurd that such accounts are on a par with our own scientifically based explanations.

But against this feeling of absurdity, you have to admit that our way of life, valuing objectivity and scientific testability as we do, is just one among many, don't you? These standards are not themselves prescribed by the world, are they? Why shouldn't there be other ways of life where what counts as an explanation — even what counts as a *reason* — is radically different from what we accept as explaining and reason-giving?

At bottom what counts is not what experiences you have, but what you make of them. Ideas, explanations, theories, and *especially* rules of procedure and standards of acceptance are not *forced* on us by the "facts." We *choose* them.

MICHAEL: I never "chose" to regard science as the best way to find out about the world.

PETER: You're right; "choice" is not quite the right word. We mature in a certain atmosphere, a certain culture; as Fred said yesterday, we more or less breathe it in as we grow up. We all grew up in the modern Western world, with its long tradition of valuing the objectivity of science. We went to school here; the prestige of science has been advertised to us since first grade.

Still, what we're talking about is analogous to a choice, because we could have developed differently; and even now, we *could choose* to give it all up and take up another way of life. Some do try to leave it all behind and live what they consider to be simpler, more natural ways of life, uncontaminated by the glories and terrors of the modern world. I think Mike himself felt that temptation at one point.

ANITA: So you think that different cultures or ways of life represent different interpretations of human experience, different "choices" humans have made as to how to construe the world they live in.

PETER: Well, isn't that the conclusion *you* are driven to when you see how all our theories and explanations of the world are *underdetermined* by the available evidence?

MICHAEL: I need to know more about this so-called "underdetermination" before I'm ready to give in.

PETER: You are a fan of modern science. So let's consider a scientific hypothesis; take a low-level one like, "Copper conducts electricity." Now, you want to say that this is based on observational evidence, right?

MICHAEL: Of course.

PETER: But you have to allow that we haven't observed all the copper there is; in fact, if you take the whole universe into account, the amount of the copper we have examined is probably a vanishingly small proportion of what there is.

MICHAEL: I guess that's so.

PETER: And yet on that basis you want to conclude that *all* copper is conductive! Isn't it obvious that there are alternative hypotheses—

such as, to be simple-minded about it, that some copper is conductive and some is not—which are completely consistent with all the observations we have made so far? That hypothesis could be *true* even though we've never found any copper that doesn't conduct electricity. Isn't that so?

MICHAEL: I suppose so.

PETER: So the hypothesis that all copper conducts electricity is not *determined* as true by the evidence we have.

ANITA: But all this shows is that you can't *deduce* the hypothesis from the evidence for it. That's hardly surprising. If I remember my philosophy right, even the early empiricists would have insisted on that.

MICHAEL: Anita is right. You have made the point that a multiplicity of hypotheses is *logically compatible* with our evidence. But that doesn't mean these two hypotheses (regarding all copper being conductive and only some being conductive) are *equally well supported* by the evidence. In fact, the hypothesis that only some copper is conductive gets *no support* at all from our observations.

ELIZABETH: You are suggesting that support is different from logical compatibility. . . . Oh, of course it is! Our evidence about copper's conductivity is *compatible* with the history of ancient Greece, but it doesn't give it any *support*.

MICHAEL: Right. This is an important distinction. It pulls the fangs from Peter's "underdetermination" argument very nicely. We can grant that theories are underdetermined by the evidence without conceding to the relativist that they are all equally well supported or equally reasonable.

PETER: Maybe. But what is this "support"?

MICHAEL: The hypothesis that all copper conducts electricity is *supported* by the evidence in that every piece of copper we have examined conducts electricity. What more do you want?

PETER: You are thinking that we observe one bit of copper, then a second, a third, and so on, noticing in each case that the copper is conductive. Then we use these observations as the premises for an *inductive argument*, whose conclusion is that *all* copper conducts electricity.

MICHAEL: That's right.

PETER: I think we are beginning to go round in circles. You tell me that it is reasonable to believe the hypothesis (call it "H") on the basis of our experience. I point out that there are alternatives, that experience is compatible with various hypotheses. You say, OK, but these alternative hypotheses aren't *supported* by the evidence the way H is supported. I ask you how H is *better supported* than its alternatives and you say—on the basis of our experience! You don't seem to see the implications of underdetermination.

ANITA: I wonder whether there may not be a better account of support available to Mike—one that is still compatible with the fact of underdetermination. That copper conducts electricity may be *suggested* to us by experience, though it can't be *proved* by experience. But on that basis we frame a universal principle that *all* copper is conductive. And then we *test* it; we try in every possible way to show it is *false*. The more tests the principle survives and the more varied the tests, the greater can be our confidence that the principle is true. Of course, we can never be absolutely certain, because the principle might fail some future test; then we could conclude that it is not as universal as we had thought.

MICHAEL: You are suggesting that our confidence in hypotheses and theories is based not on a positive inductive argument for them, but on the failure of our attempts to falsify them. I like that. It takes Peter's underdetermination thesis neatly into account and yet explains how we can rationally have more confidence in some theories than in others. On this understanding, the hypothesis that some copper conducts electricity and some doesn't fares miserably.

PETER: I'm not sure that gets you out of the soup completely. You always have an option to reject any particular test as an anomaly and hang on to the hypothesis. Scientists will sometimes say, "That just *can't* be right!" Whether you accept the results or reject them comes down again in the end to a decision—and that means to preferences.

But there's an even deeper reason why there are always alternative accounts of our experience. As I noted earlier, uninterpreted experience is dumb; it says nothing. So even our reports of *observations* are permeated with interpretations. And that is obvious once you see that they have to be framed in language.

ANITA: The results of tests obviously have to be reported in language. But I don't see what that's going to get you.

PETER: Think about it this way. Every language divides up the world in a certain way—and not all alike, either. The concepts expressible in one language may not match up at all neatly with those in another. So there are *no neutral observations*; even the most basic observations are *contaminated*. And what they are contaminated with are interpretations.

It's as though every language embodies a set of hypotheses or theories about the world: what sorts of things there are, how they should be classified, how they are related to each other.

MICHAEL: I hate to be repetitive, but what's the point?

PETER: You want to say that theories are not all on a par because some are better supported by tests. But there are no neutral tests. And in fact observations are framed in terms borrowed from theories—often from the very theories they are supposed to test. To claim that one theory can be more reasonable than another because it is "supported by experience" is to suppose that experience can be talked about in a kind of theory-neutral language. And there isn't any such language.

Sam says that he accepts the testimony of those who wrote the Bible because his own experience corroborates what they say. But isn't it overwhelmingly likely that the language in which he interprets his experience is itself shaped by the Christian tradition? If so, it's not a very independent appeal, and it can't give much support.

FRED: Hear, hear!

PETER: I don't want it to look like I'm picking on Sam, so let's take a very different example. It may seem to Western scientists as though there were a neutral ground on which to build, but that is just because they are so familiar with the interpretations foisted on their experience by their tradition and language. It's a lack of imagination on their part.

There isn't any bedrock for knowledge, no neutral ground on which we can build our foundations; it's unstable all the way down.

ANITA: I remember a striking analogy that goes like this: "We are like sailors out on the open sea who cannot put into dry dock to repair their ship out of the best materials—but have to repair it nonetheless!"[5]

PETER: That's the idea. The ship is the system of our beliefs—what keeps us from drowning in the turbulence of the world. It's made up of our firm convictions, our theories, our guesses, our hunches. We can test and revise them, but only from on board. Just as the sailors have to stand on their ship to repair it, we are always taking theories for granted in tinkering with them.

SAM: Can't there be more than one ship?

PETER: That's exactly what I've been trying to get you to see. There are *many* ships!

SAM: But each of us is stuck on one?

PETER: For the most part. But you *can* jump ship—leap on to another one, as it were. That's what it would be like if you convinced Michael to accept Christianity. Or if he persuaded you to give it up and see things his way. I think you call it *conversion*. There aren't any good reasons for it. All the *reasons* are on board one ship or another.

SAM: You mentioned persuasion yesterday. If I can't find *good reasons* to get Michael onto my ship, how could I persuade him?

5. W. V. Quine takes this aphorism from Otto Neurath as a motto for his book, *Word and Object* (The MIT Press, 1960): "Wie Schiffer sind wir, die ihr Schiff auf offener See umbauen müssen, ohne es jemals in einem Dock zerlegen und aus besten Bestandteilen neu errichten zu können."

PETER: Oh, I don't know. Different techniques might work for different people. How do advertisers get you to want their products? How do politicians get you to vote for them? How do effective preachers like Billy Graham do their thing? One way or another Mike would have to experience a kind of "gestalt switch," like the one you experience when you switch from seeing the vase to seeing the two faces. You must be familiar with the example. It looks like this.

(Draws)

MICHAEL: So you want to say that all the reasons we could have for changing our views are already a part of some view or other; if that's so, it looks like rationality itself is relative to particular views or frameworks—or whatever you want to call a kind of global picture of things.

PETER: Can you see any alternative? If you move from one "ship" to another, it's like gaining a new perspective on things, like *seeing* things in an altogether different way. Even what counts as a reason, what is taken to be evidence, would look different on board a different ship. If you board Sam's ship through some sort of conversion, you will have reasons for your beliefs that didn't look like reasons before.

But there's nothing *rational* about the switch itself. You either see the two faces or you don't.

ANITA: That sort of conversion certainly happens. It *may* even happen in the sciences occasionally, when one global theory replaces another—though I believe that's controversial.

But I have a few questions.

PETER: You always do.

ANITA: The image of ships is very dramatic, but I wonder whether it doesn't have just the same shortcomings as Fred's earlier appeal to cultures. Isn't it in fact the same claim in picturesque form? The problem again is identifying the ship you are on, together with the probability that we are all sailing on numerous ships at the same time.

PETER: I don't see what the problem is even if you're right. So what if we aren't confined to one ship?

ANITA: It's very important. You were arguing earlier that observations are contaminated by the very theories they are designed to test. You concluded that tests are worthless – that they can't do the job of supporting a theory because they are "co-opted" by the theory they are supposed to test. If that were so, the result would be a kind of cognitive isolation that the image of the ship seems to reinforce.

But what this image ignores is that we can test one theory or belief by relying on observations framed in language related to *other* theories – theories *independent* of the first.

MICHAEL: That's right. If we want to test the hypothesis that copper conducts electricity, we may need to rely on some general theories about electricity and about the instruments which measure it. But we aren't relying on that hypothesis itself.

ANITA: So even if there isn't any *neutral ground* to stand on, it doesn't follow that we are condemned to be always begging the question.

MICHAEL: In terms of the image, the sailors might stand on a lower deck to repair a higher one. And, come to think of it, they could later rely on the higher one to rebuild the lower.

ANITA: Exactly. Or they could even stand on one ship while working on a second.

MICHAEL: If that's right, then tests of theories don't all have to be question-begging or circular. (Though maybe some are.) Our experience can give us genuine evidence, and so genuine support, even if there is no absolutely neutral language in which to frame it.

ANITA: And if that's right, then it can be reasonable to accept one theory rather than another.

ELIZABETH: I wonder, though, whether it's even true that there is no neutral language to appeal to in testing our beliefs.

ANITA: How do you mean?

ELIZABETH: Well, think of reports of what we see, of just using language to describe what we observe.

PETER: There seems to be a lot of psychological evidence that we see what we expect to see. We are primed to see certain things and not others, and to interpret them in terms of our belief structure. To turn an old phrase around, *believing is seeing*. Or, as some philosophers say, *all seeing is seeing as*. . . . And what you see something *as* is determined by your theories or views of things in general—*not* by what's before your eyes.

ELIZABETH: There is that phenomenon, of course. But I wonder whether it hasn't got limits. You can "prime" someone to see the vase in your figure by telling them you are going to show them a vase picture, or by showing them this picture in a series of vase pictures. But it would be hard to get someone to see it as a mosquito or a Kansas wheat field. The thing just *resists* certain interpretations.

ANITA: You think observations can have an independence of our theories? I don't know. . . .

ELIZABETH: I think there is enough independence to make total theory-relativity a myth. If observations were completely open to higher-level cognitive manipulation, it would be hard to explain some things.
    Peter, you gave us an ambiguous picture which can be seen one way or another, depending, perhaps, on cognitive anticipations.

But how about the illusion of the two lines that look to be of different lengths? You know the one I mean.

(Draws)

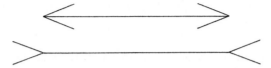

We believe firmly that the two lines are exactly the same length (we may have measured them); and we can even know the psychological explanation for the illusion that one looks longer. But it doesn't make any difference; they still *look* like they aren't the same.

MICHAEL: I don't see the point.

ELIZABETH: It's just that here we have a case where what something is *seen as* is absolutely resistant to even the firmest theoretical convictions. No matter how hard we try, we just can't see these two lines the way we know they really are.

FRED: You're not trying to tell us that our "knowledge" in this case is in error, are you?

ELIZABETH: No, not at all. But Peter's arguments seem to depend on there being *no resistance* to interpretation in our observations. He talks as though we could see *anything as anything*. What the example shows is that our observational capacities are not as malleable as all that; if they were, then we should all be able to see the lines as equal, since that is what we all believe them to be. Another example is the movies. We all know that what we are really seeing is a rapidly displayed series of still shots; but no matter how firmly you believe that, there is no way you can see it that way.

If perceptual capacities are at least partly isolated from cognitive influence, it follows that observation can be more or less neutral as between theories, something people with different views can have in common, and something to appeal to in making rational decisions between theories. At the very least it seems that Peter's style of argument presupposes a certain psychological theory about perception. And this theory may not be a true one.[6]

SAM: So you three think Peter's arguments haven't proved his relativistic beliefs.

PETER: But I'm not trying to prove relativism is true. I'm just trying to get you to see that a clear-headed appreciation of things you already believe will leave you in a relativistic situation. By that I mean you will have to admit that you can't demonstrate one global view is better than another.

ANITA: But so far you haven't done that, Peter. You point out that our evidence underdetermines our beliefs; and we all agree. But it doesn't follow from this that all our beliefs are equally good, because it doesn't follow that they have all passed equally stringent tests.

You point out that there is no neutral evidence to appeal to for support, since the language in which the evidence is framed contains interpretive elements. Liz doesn't seem to agree. But even those of us who are inclined to see it that way don't see that your conclusion follows; the evidence may not be "contaminated" (as you put it) by just those theories we are testing.

So far we have no reason to give up our natural conviction that some beliefs are better than others and can be shown to be so.

MICHAEL: I agree with Anita. Nothing you've said so far shows that science can't get us the truth about the world. Sure, any one of our theories might be mistaken. But progress is possible. We can get better and better theories. And we can revise our language, too, if that's necessary. In fact, scientists are notorious for inventing new words for new ideas to reflect newly discovered realities.

6. An argument like Elizabeth's is made by Jerry Fodor in terms of the "cognitive impenetrability" of the "module" of perception. Jerry Fodor, "Observation Reconsidered," *A Theory of Content* (The MIT Press, 1990). He adds, apropos of the sort of argument Peter is running, "Granny says that a little psychology is a dangerous thing and inclineth a man to relativism" (ibid, p. 243).

PETER: I'm sorry, but you don't seem to grasp the full implications of what you say you have accepted. Michael's use of the word "reflect" is an example of that obtuseness. The word is a metaphor and comes from the world of mirrors and still lakes which can reflect or show back just what is there. But language isn't like that. To put it another way, there's always a *conventional* element in our languages, and so in our theories as well. Something we supply. None of them are mirrors of reality; they reflect as much about us as about the world. They show our interests, our desires, our traditions—our *customs*, to come back again to where we started.

ELIZABETH: It's clearly a matter of convention whether we measure distances in meters or yards, kilometers or miles. Is that what you mean?

PETER: That's an example.

ELIZABETH: But that kind of conventionality is no barrier to knowing the truth about the world. If I say that our ride tomorrow is 50 miles long, I suppose that reflects something about me. A German or New Zealander might say the distance is about 80 kilometers. But we are both saying the same thing about the distance; and what each of us says is true.

ANITA: Certainly languages divide up the world in different ways. And differences in language reflect differences in our interests, just as Peter says. Skiers distinguish varieties of snow that I can't tell apart. But that doesn't mean that what I call "snow" isn't snow. Or that somehow my belief that it snows in Vermont in the winter is less than perfectly true. It may be less *precise* than what a skier is equipped to say, but that's a different matter.

PETER: Well, I can see that these arguments are not doing the trick. But maybe that's because they are being considered one by one. If you think of them all together, and especially in the light of the most powerful argument, which I am now going to remind you of, I think you will see that you have no conclusive reason to prefer any view, theory, or belief to any other.

MICHAEL: I tremble.

PETER: Think back to the little exchange between Sam and Michael. What came out clearly was that they differ about the appropriate *standards* for belief acceptance. Mike wants us to accept only beliefs we can test against the senses; Sam's test is ultimately the authority of the Bible. Am I right so far?

SAM: Not quite. I have nothing against science and its methods of testing hypotheses. As a dentist I rely on what we have come to know that way about teeth and diseases of the mouth. I just don't think science is *enough*. Science doesn't save souls.

ELIZABETH: What do you mean?

SAM: Well, the scientists I have known are, on the whole, no better than most people. No worse either, I suppose. But for all their scientific expertise, they can be as selfish, arrogant, unkind, and heartless as you can imagine. There's nothing in the rules or practice of science that even questions these character traits. I want something more than that, something that challenges that way of life and inspires us to higher things.

MICHAEL: If you think all scientists are evil monsters, you are sadly mistaken. A scientist can have as demanding a code of ethics as you might like.

SAM: But he doesn't get it from his science. That's my point.

FRED: I don't see that religion is any great source of virtue. Don't forget Peter's reminder of the harm that "good" people have done.

PETER: I'm afraid we're in danger of getting off the track here. The crucial point remains that Sam thinks it legitimate, right, or appropriate to appeal to a certain standard for belief that Mike denies.

Now, let's ask Mike whether among the rules of good scientific procedure—formulate theories that have wide application, that are testable, fruitful, simple, and so on—there is a rule that says: accept the rules of science as your standard of belief.

MICHAEL: I think that's just good sense.

PETER: But that doesn't answer my question. Is it or is it not one of the rules of science that we should appeal to the rules of science to settle our beliefs?

MICHAEL: Hmmm. I see what you are driving at. I don't suppose it is. If it were, then it would have force only for those who already accepted science as the standard. And they wouldn't need it.

PETER: So the choice to accept this standard for belief is *external* to science. But if that's so, then Michael *can't* just be relying on science as a measure of belief. He's relying on a *non*-scientific rule which says to accept scientific rules for belief-acceptance.

MICHAEL: But there is a kind of objectivity in the procedures of science—and in the results it produces.

PETER: Even if that is so, we need to ask whether the same objectivity attaches to the choice to value objectivity. Is your choice to put a high value on objectivity itself an *objective* choice? Or isn't it rather purely subjective, merely a matter of your own preferences?

As far as I can see, the *preference* for objectivity in beliefs is just another tribal tradition.

MICHAEL: But that would make science just another *ideology*—no more valid than any other!

PETER: Michael, you have said it.

SAM: That would put my religion and my science on the same footing. I like that. But I'm not sure I like where it leaves either one of them.

PETER: You may not like it, but exactly the same argument applies to you. It can't be a rule *in* the Bible which says that you should use the Bible as the standard against which to test beliefs. If there were such a Biblical rule it would create such a tight little circle you couldn't hope ever to break in to it.

ANITA: I see what you are saying. The rule would tell us: accept what the Bible teaches. And if you ask, "Why should I accept this rule?" the answer is . . .

PETER: Because it's what the Bible teaches. But if I ask why I should accept what the Bible teaches, the answer is . . .

ANITA: Because this rule says so. And around and around you go.

PETER: But, and this is the important part, this circularity doesn't put that particular standard at any disadvantage in comparison with any other. *No* such rule can be justified in a non-circular way. And Sam's choice is just as "rational" as Mike's—or any other, including the choices of those cultures that interpret storms in terms of the wills of gods and spirits.

MICHAEL: I still don't see how that can be as *rational* as explaining storms by the scientific principles of modern meteorology.

PETER: Here we come back to the point we discussed earlier; but now it has more punch to it. Accepting certain standards for belief is equivalent to accepting a certain kind of rationality. The standards tell you what there are *good reasons* to believe. I wager that Sam, for instance, thinks it is perfectly rational to believe that Jesus is the Son of God. Why? Because there is a good reason to believe it—the authority of the scriptures. What you haven't yet grasped clearly is that there are *alternative rationalities,* just as there are alternative cultures or customs. Rationality is a matter of custom, too.

ANITA: So you think the issue of standards for belief, and even standards of rationality itself, comes down to a kind of blind, irrational choice.

PETER: As we said earlier, "choice" is not quite the right word. But it has the right flavor.
    As for "irrational," I would rather say these "choices" are *non*-rational or *pre*-rational. To call them *ir*-rational is to use a term of criticism, and there's nothing *wrong* with them. We all make such choices—and can't help it.

SAM: If you are right, it seems very important for us that we make *good* choices.

PETER: I'm afraid, Sam, you still haven't seen the point. Criteria of goodness, just like standards of rationality, are *internal* to those points of view we leap into when we "choose" in this way. The notion that we can decide, from some independent, neutral, objective standpoint which choices are good ones is a will-o'-the-wisp. Fred was quite right about that yesterday.

ANITA: So this is your relativism.

PETER: That's it. Let me remind you that I haven't been trying to *assert* that everything is relative, either to an individual or a culture. I've been trying to *show* you that things you already believe should make you realize that our situation is incurably relativistic. You might say I've just been assembling reminders of what you all know, but haven't taken sufficiently into account.[7]

Our views of the world, and even our best scientific theories, are underdetermined by the evidence, the evidence itself is not neutral but contaminated by our theories, our language is not a mirror of reality but manifests our interests and desires, and to cap it all off, the standards we apply—the very rules of rationality itself— are matters for which no good reasons can be given, since these standards themselves determine what counts as a good reason. Maybe none of these considerations alone convince you, but taken together, how can there be any doubt?

That's just the human predicament. And without ceasing to be human, there's no getting out of it.

ELIZABETH: Well, you've given us all a lot to think about, Peter. Our minds are likely to be as active as our legs tomorrow. Or maybe—maybe we've said everything there is to say on this topic and tomorrow night we'll have to find another.

ANITA: I can't frame them just now, but I have this feeling that by tomorrow night I'll have some questions for Peter.

ALL: (groan)

PETER: In the meantime, here's a question for you all. I've tried to show you that we are caught in a relativistic predicament. That's

7. "The work of the philosopher consists in assembling reminders for a particular purpose" (Ludwig Wittgenstein, *Philosophical Investigations* 127 [Basil Blackwell, 1958]).

the conclusion clear thinking has to come to, no matter where it starts. But if you don't like that conclusion, let me ask you: What's the alternative?

FRED: Since I, of course, don't think there is one, I will feel free to let my mind wander tomorrow. The rest of you can try to anticipate Anita's questions and meet Peter's challenge. I wish you luck.

MICHAEL: We may need some luck on the road tomorrow, too. I understand the route takes us over a mountain pass. And the weather also seems primed to make things hard for us. The forecast is for wind and storms.

ELIZABETH: All of which suggests we had better get our rest. Goodnight all. See you in the morning.

The Third Conversation

The Evening of Their Fourth Day Together

ELIZABETH: I'm glad we decided to stick together on our ride today. More or less anyway.

SAM: Me too. I suppose it was a little hard on you and Michael, having to go so slow. How did you get to be so quick on a bike?

ELIZABETH: I raced for a few years. Before I was married. I enjoyed the challenge. It stretches you.

PETER: *I* enjoyed having witnesses this afternoon to the fact that I rode every inch of the way.

MICHAEL: So you did! But I can't decide whether it was more humorous or more painful to watch you weaving back and forth across the road on the long climb. Good thing there wasn't much traffic.

PETER: I suffered. But I was not defeated.

ANITA: Not yet, anyway. I did think of a few questions to ask you.

FRED: Oh, oh. Here it comes. The cross-examination.

MICHAEL: Before we get to that part of the program, could I say something?

ANITA: Sure. We gave Fred a second chance last night and we can do the same for you. My questions aren't going to disappear.

MICHAEL: It has to do with Peter's claim that science is just another ideology, that objectivity is merely a personal preference. Now I just have a real hard time swallowing that. And as I was thinking about it today, I thought I could see why.

53

SAM: Let's hear it. I'm not in love with this way of putting science and religion on a par either—as just personal prejudices. I want to save them *both* from such a fate.

MICHAEL: Well, you'll have to fight the religion battle on your own, Sam. But as for science, I think we have good reason to reject Peter's view of it. There's a fact about science that Pete doesn't take into account: it works.

To understand the significance of that, we have to begin with the fact that we live in a world we didn't make. Whatever this world is, it has a reality quite independent of us. It existed before there were any humans in it and it will be here long after humans are gone. That mountain we climbed this afternoon is just one example.

Most certainly, then, the world is independent of our *minds*—of what we think of it, of our theories about it.

SAM: That's like your point the first night about the bike tubing; whether it is strong enough for a strong rider doesn't depend on whether we think it is. Thinking so doesn't make it so.

MICHAEL: But we have to live in this world of independent realities. So it's important for us to have true beliefs about it. How we act depends, at least in part, on what we believe about the situation we are in.

ELIZABETH: You mean like this afternoon. We all stopped to put our rain gear on when that storm blew in.

MICHAEL: Right. We did that because we *believed* it was about to rain. Since that was a *true* belief, acting on it kept us from getting wet.

PETER: From getting *too* wet, you mean.

MICHAEL: Sure. But if we hadn't acted on that belief we would have gotten soaked. And cold. And maybe gotten pneumonia.

So anyway, what we want, to be able to live in this world, is true beliefs about it. Without true beliefs about what foods are safe, we might just as easily eat the poisonous things and avoid the nourishing things. And that would be the end of us.

PETER: Suppose we grant this—though I am not likely to. What do you think you can get from it?

MICHAEL: Science is nothing more than a set of techniques for getting true beliefs about the world. It is our *best* method for doing that. In fact, nothing else has ever come close.

That's why you have this remarkable spread of science all over the world. People from nearly every culture on earth recognize this, and they want to be in on it.

PETER: Your "spread of science" seems to me just the last gasp of Western imperialism. That's a tradition with a long history, you know: foisting *our* ways on the natives. It's a pretty dismal history, too. Most of the natives are just saying, "Leave us alone."

MICHAEL: Of course lots of terrible things were done, probably are still being done in this ethnocentric way. But it just doesn't seem true that we are "foisting" our science on the rest of the world. Look at our graduate schools—especially in the sciences and engineering. They're graduating more PhD's from Asia and Africa and South America and the Middle East than from our own country. Science education is our most successful export!

And we don't have to *market* it; students are clamoring to get in—often supported by their governments. Why?

FRED: Because they all want to drive BMW's.

MICHAEL: That may be part of it, but I don't think it is the main reason. It's because science puts us in command of *truths* about the world. With its help we know what will happen if we act on the world in this way or that. Science gives us the *knowledge* to cure diseases, improve crop yield, invent the telephone, the radio, the computer, send satellites into the sky . . .

ANITA: . . . pollute the rivers, foul the air, threaten the world with nuclear destruction . . .

MICHAEL: Yes, yes, I know. We haven't *used* all this knowledge very well. But knowledge is power. And it's this promise of *control* that attracts people to science. Why is it that our children aren't dying from polio any more, or being paralyzed by it? It's because Jonas Salk and Albert Sabin used the power of their knowledge about viruses and antibodies to develop a polio vaccine that protects children from this deadly disease. Cases went from 20,000 per year down to essentially zero.

ELIZABETH: Not in some Asian and African countries, as I understand it.

MICHAEL: Right. But that is just more evidence for the *effectiveness* of cures based on science; where the science is lacking—or governments are unwilling to use it in constructive ways—so are the cures. Science works!

Take another example. Peter wants to say that explaining storms in personal terms is as good as explaining them scientifically. Now we all know that scientific weather forecasting isn't perfect. But when the forecasting equipment on Samoa broke down some time back and they couldn't predict the course of an approaching hurricane, many people died needlessly. Does Peter really think a shaman could have stepped in to do the job equally well?

Science just isn't like astrology or a belief in spirits controlling the storms. It tells us the truth about the world.

PETER: Very eloquent, Mike—but hardly likely to convince. You say science tells us "the truth" about the world; but we all know that "science" changes its mind all the time. Just read the science writers, week after week, trying to keep us up to date on the latest changes in opinion about the composition of the universe, or subatomic particles or, for that matter, what you should eat to avoid heart trouble.

The history of science has been a story of junking one theory after another. The only warranted inference is that what science tells you today is *true*, it will tell you tomorrow is *false!*

MICHAEL: Of course scientists change their minds—especially about things on the frontiers of knowledge. But that's one of the *strengths* of science. It means we are rejecting theories that looked good but are now seen to be flawed. That's how we get better, truer theories.

In my own field there are lots of theories that are pretty well settled, though some are more speculative. And there are loads of other truths that don't usually count as "theories," truths we just rely on every day. Think about the principle of the lever, which has been around unchanged since Archimedes proved the theorem that governs it in the third century BC.

ANITA: The fact that you rely on these principles doesn't mean they are *true*, Mike. About that Peter is right. It just means you find them *useful*.

MICHAEL: I don't think so. We apply these theories to build machines. And the *machines* work. Now if the theories aren't true, what explains their *success* when applied?

It's like saying, "Pushing on that shift lever will get you into a lower gear." You can think of that as a mini-theory, if you like; it applies to every such lever on every bike in good condition. Well, you push it and—yep! There you are, in a lower gear. The fact that it works when you act on it *shows* that it is true.

Moreover, if you push the lever and you *don't* get the gear you want, you know something is wrong. And the way to correct it is not to appeal to the gods to make it right, but to do some quasi-scientific investigation to find out where the mechanism has broken down. You frame a hypothesis that it might be a loose wire. You test it. If it's not that, you frame another hypothesis and conduct your test. When you find the problem, you fix it. Science in a nutshell. It works. And why? Because the hypotheses and theories it leads us to are true of this world we live in. Our theories are useful *because* they are true.

PETER: But false theories can work, too.

SAM: How's that?

PETER: If I'm not mistaken, scientists believe that Einsteinian physics is a more adequate description of the universe than Newton's.

MICHAEL: Right.

PETER: But for several centuries, Newton's principles "worked" very well. They gave quite accurate predictions about all sorts of things—not only the tides and the fall of apples. And for most ordinary purposes Newtonian physics still works well enough. It's a lot simpler, so why bother with the mathematical complexities if you don't have to?

MICHAEL: Newtonian physics works as well as it does because it is a good *approximation* of the truth.

ANITA: But I think that gives the game away, Mike. You want to say that science works because it's true. Peter's example shows that truth is not necessary to have beliefs that work. And it is easy to think up other examples. Suppose you are shipwrecked on a strange island and you don't know what to eat. You try eating this plant and that. You get sick and you formulate the hypothesis that it is plants of a certain sort that are responsible. So you avoid them. Avoiding them works; you no longer get sick.

But in fact that variety includes two sub-species; one makes you sick and the other—the most plentiful variety on the island—is extremely delicious and nourishing. So your belief works to keep you from getting sick, but it is false.

MICHAEL: But the cure for that is more science! You may be afraid to do the experimentation, but if you *could* do it you would learn the truth. And that would work even better.

ANITA: Nonetheless, at any moment in the history of science, there is no way we can distinguish between the cases where we have the truth about the world and cases like my example. So you can't defend science as the way to get true beliefs on the basis that it works. *That* just doesn't work!

PETER: I wonder whether there isn't an even deeper problem with this attempt to defend science. You want to appeal to what works. But the very idea of "working" has reference to some aim or end in view. What works is what serves your *interests*. Your shifter "works" when it does what you *want* it to do.

If anything is obvious, it is that people's wants vary tremendously—not only individually, but culturally, too. Science may *not* work—for a certain culture—if what people in that culture most want is not the sort of thing that science can deliver. That's why science is not *absolutely* superior to other ways of forming beliefs—for instance, accepting the words of one's wise ancestors. It's all relative to what you want.

MICHAEL: But that ignores the independence of the world we live in. As I see it, human beings—all human beings—have certain interests in common. We *all* want to survive and prosper in a world not of our own making. To do that we need to know as accurately as we can what this world is like. And, despite what you say, there is nothing like science to tell us that. Listening to the ancestors just doesn't compete.

PETER: I hate to sound like a broken record, but you keep making assumptions that just show your ethnocentrism. You appeal to what "works," and when I point out that ideas of "working" vary with cultures you claim that everyone wants to "survive and prosper." But don't you see that the same point can be made with respect to these concepts?
What do people *mean* by "prospering"? You assume it involves control over nature. But maybe some people aren't interested in controlling nature; they just want to live peaceably in harmony with their environment. Your reliance on such notions in defending science as a mode of successful control over nature is just an example of typical Western materialism.

MICHAEL: And *you* are so in the grip of relativistic notions that you can't acknowledge what is obvious—the common interests humans have with respect to the world we live in. There are lots of variations, sure; but no one, anywhere, prefers debilitating illness to health, the early death of their children to a long life for them, starvation to a full belly, famine to plenty, loneliness to communication with distant loved ones. And so on.

You want to make everything relative to interests. But you ignore the fact that there is one interest human beings all share—an interest in the truth about the world. And this common interest can be satisfied better by science than by any other method of inquiry. Bar none.

SAM: I am sympathetic to that point of view myself. But Peter and Anita have put forward some pretty strong arguments. Is there anything else you can say in defense of it?

MICHAEL: Sure. We can ask *why* science is so much better at explaining and predicting the course of the world. The reason is that science is just the systematic development of a common-sense technique for letting the world have a say in the formation of our beliefs. An experiment is like a question put to the world: Is this the way you are? And the world answers yes or no.

PETER: Don't be so naive, Michael! We agreed last night that our *senses* don't *tell us* anything. And the *world* doesn't *say* anything either! It's up to us what to make of any experiment, and there are always alternatives. Most of the quarrels among scientists concern what significance to assign to experimental results. That is, how they should be *interpreted*.

And we also agreed that our theories are underdetermined by the evidence. So *no* experiment could *force* any particular theory on us. What theories we prefer are as much a function of our interests and goals as of the way the world is.

MICHAEL: OK, OK. I didn't put that very well. That *was* naive. And I want to admit everything you just said, but with a little change of emphasis. You say our theories are as much a function of our interests as they are of the world. I want to say that theories in science—and this is what makes science more than just another ideology—are as much a function of the way the world is as they are of our interests and desires.

What makes science different is, perhaps, a matter of degree. It's not that in science the world by itself *fixes* our beliefs; you are right about that. But the methods of science are designed precisely to allow the world to *matter more* in the formation of beliefs than any other method allows. The techniques of scientific investigation are set up to allow the world itself to play a role in filtering out mistaken interpretations.

Everyone is interested in the truth about the world, and science satisfies that interest better than any other method. And why? Because it is the only way humans have found to minimize (not get rid of, but minimize) their own personal and cultural biases about the world. That's the sort of objectivity you can get in science. And that's why people all over the world prize it. Given our common interest in getting along in this world we didn't make, science is a better method of belief acquisition than any other.

You wanted an alternative to your everything-is-equally-interpretation sort of relativism, Peter? Well, here is one, and a powerful one, too.

PETER: I don't think I am defeated yet. Scientists are human, too, right?

MICHAEL: Of course.

PETER: And they have their own interests and desires?

MICHAEL: Sure. But I don't see what you are driving at.

PETER: Think about the young assistant professor of chemistry. Does she want tenure at her university? Oh yes—take it from me!—she does. Will this influence the direction of her research? Oh yes, it will.

Take the senior chemist in her department. Will he (not likely to be a "she" yet) direct his research so as to get his grants from the funding agency renewed? Oh yes, he will.

Consider a biologist who is deeply religious in a conservative denomination. Will he be inclined to look for flaws in evolutionary theory? Oh yes, he will. And is he likely to think he has found them? Well, I leave you to answer that.

ANITA: You are pointing out that scientists have all sorts of interests which are not strictly scientific. That's no doubt true; we all have to pay the bills. But are you suggesting that these interests play a significant role in which theories are accepted?

PETER: Indeed I am. Science is a social system like any other. And the desire of scientists for approval by their peers (or their religious communities), for promotions, salary raises, and Nobel prizes shape the products of this system as much as any other.

Take the case of Lord Kelvin, a famous physicist, but also conventionally devout, "proving" that the earth was not old enough for biological evolution to have occurred.

FRED: Ha! Peter made it up the mountain by weaving across the road from side to side. I see he is equally adept at weaving through the threads of Mike's argument.

MICHAEL: But this time, I think he won't make it to the top! The influence of extra-scientific motivations on scientists can't be denied. But consider the Kelvin case. He was indeed a distinguished scientist, and he may have been motivated in part by religious considerations. But he had very strong *scientific* reasons for his conclusions as well. And though it was influential for a while, his "proof" did not become a part of accepted science because it depended on not knowing about radioactivity as a source of heat. When that was discovered, the scientific basis for his conclusions disappeared, and so did his "proof."

The moral of this little story is that science is more than the beliefs of individual scientists. In fact, the social system of science — its structure of rewards, for instance — is set up so that mistakes due to the influence of these non-scientific factors are eventually filtered out. Science is a social activity, and an important part of it is trying to show where errors have been made. Even if individual scientists are not eager to discover their own mistakes, they always have to worry about other investigators turning them up. Science is a long-term, world-wide enterprise. And the errors of individuals tend to be canceled out by the system.

SAM: If you put this consideration about the *social system of science* together with your earlier point about the *role the world itself plays* in the selection of scientific theories, I think you may have a strong case for the non-relativistic status of science.

PETER: But even if the prejudices of individuals can be filtered out by the methods of science (and I am dubious about that), the *choice* of scientific standards for belief — as against any number of other alternatives — is still purely subjective. That was my point yesterday evening. So I don't think I am defeated yet!

ANITA: Well, it so happens that that is exactly what I wanted to ask you about.

FRED: Here we go again!

ANITA: You want to say, Peter, that we are forced to "choose" standards for believing, and that this choice can't be rationally justified. The reason it can't be rationally justified is that what *counts* as being rational (and even what counts as giving a reason) is *defined* by the standard chosen. So we can't, without begging the question, give a reason for choosing one standard rather than another.

Do I understand you correctly?

PETER: That's the argument in a nutshell.

ANITA: Even choosing "   ssible, would therefore express a merel   erence?

PETER: Right again.

ANITA: Well, my first ques   rry we have already seen—twice, I think   xive card." I don't want to put too much   nk it should be mentioned. In this little ar   s *reasons* for a conclusion. The conclusion is supposed to be a relativistic one. But are these reasons themselves relative to a framework that defines what reasons are to be?

MICHAEL: Ah yes, by now we can all see how this goes. If they are relative to a framework, then how can they establish the relativistic conclusion absolutely?

SAM: And if they are not, then they assume a kind of absolute rationality.

MICHAEL: Though then there would have to be something wrong with the argument!

PETER: Yes, yes. We all know these little dialectical games. Actually, I find them a bit tiresome. Let me remind you that I am not defending a *position* called "relativism," but trying to get you to see that you yourselves have no way to avoid the relativistic predicament we are all in. I wasn't so much *endorsing* that argument, as asking whether *you* don't have to accept it. On your *own* terms.

ANITA: I thought you might say that; that's why I didn't want to put too much stress on it. So let me go on to the second question, which should address exactly that point. I think we may begin to see the outlines of another alternative to relativism, too.

How *realistic* is the picture of our intellectual life that you sketch for us? You argue that rational judgments are restricted to a framework which defines what a reason is to be. There are many such frameworks, you say, so there are many rationalities. The choice of one rather than another can't, then, be a matter of having reasons to choose that one.

PETER: As far as I can see, it comes down to personal preference.

ANITA: And judgments that one set of standards or a certain kind of rationality is *better* than another must be similar.

PETER: In the last analysis, yes. You will remember that I argued the first night that we could make evaluative judgments about others who didn't share our standards (about Sam, for instance, in the little dentist story); but I didn't say there was anything *rational* about that. What grounds are you going to appeal to if you want to say one *standard of goodness or rationality* is better than another?

ANITA: That sounds like a powerful argument. But I think it sounds strong only because it is so *abstract*. It's not only abstract, but unrealistic, too. So far as I can see, you haven't given us a *description* of our human form of life, but something more like a *template* laid on top of it. You then read your argument off the lines of the template and think you are describing what it is laid on.

ELIZABETH: Anita has a point. You seem to picture our intellectual life as if it were an axiom system in mathematics. Our ordinary beliefs, or scientific theories, are like theorems and the standards are like axioms. You imagine different people or different cultures as embodiments of different axioms; their different beliefs are the consequences. People can only have the beliefs their standards permit.

Now you can't deduce theorems in geometry from axioms that are suitable only for arithmetic. So if you want to move from doing arithmetic to doing geometry, you have to get a whole new set of principles. Analogously, your picture allows us only to change beliefs *radically* by a kind of non-rational conversion to another set of axioms. But is our life really like that?

MICHAEL: I see what Anita and Liz are getting at. If we accept the picture of our cognitive life Peter offers us, the only way we could *rationally* say one set of standards is better than another is from some point of view outside both of them.

ELIZABETH: But even then you couldn't say the point of view you occupied was better than the one you were evaluating—without begging the question. So you would have *no reason* to *rely* on judgments from that point of view either.

If our comparative judgments of goodness are going to be rational, Peter's argument seems to drive us to that "view from nowhere" we mentioned earlier. But we all agreed that was impossible.

PETER: I'm delighted that you see our predicament so clearly!

ANITA: Let me rephrase my point of a moment ago. What we see so clearly is a certain *schema* for interpreting our lives. It obviously has a fascination. We are imagined to be ideal knowers, tightly organized little packages of wholly consistent information, isolated and immune from contamination. But when we look carefully at how we actually form our beliefs, discuss moral issues, and learn from one another, we can see that this schema *distorts* the realities tremendously.

There's a funny sort of irony here. It was Peter who last night was pushing the idea that all our beliefs and theories are interpretations. In a way, I think we should accept that. But his *version* of "its all interpretation" is itself an interpretation. And I'm confident there is *good reason* to reject it—which is just what his version says I couldn't have.

The big problem with this picture, Peter, is that it makes rationality so rigid, so static, . . . so *rationalistic*. It's as if you relativists inherited a concept of REASON modeled on mathematics—one that was supposed to prove truths with certainty. When it became obvious that it couldn't do that outside of very restricted spheres, you *could* have said, "Well, we have learned reason isn't that kind of thing." But what you do instead is nostalgically hang on to that old concept and despair over its shortcomings. All that is left, then, are non-rational desires, personal preferences, and power relations.

ELIZABETH: I think Anita is right. You relativists are like disappointed lovers who can't get over it. Instead of sensibly settling in with a decent, hard-working wife, you keep mooning about the beautiful princess you can't have. If you can't have certainty, you are determined to have nothing!

MICHAEL: It's as though only *everything* could possibly be enough.

ANITA: Right. But I think we have to say that enough is enough.[8] And we do have enough to judge reasonably among different standards of rationality and goodness. At least in some cases.

PETER: Do you think you have a better interpretation of our lives? You seemed to suggest you had an alternative.

ANITA: Well, I come at it from an altogether different angle. I think our lives are much messier than this tidied-up picture suggests — and much more interesting and fruitful, too. For one thing, patterns of belief are not static in either individuals or cultures. They are always under pressures of various kinds and always changing as a result. Patterns crystallize for a time, some of them more fixed than others. And some of them last a long time. But there is scarcely one of them that isn't subject to change.

MICHAEL: That seems right. In fact there is a word for a person who is absolutely immune to change: fanatic.

ANITA: And our standards for belief acceptance change, too. Peter wants to say that they can only change by a kind of non-rational revolution, where everything left behind is repudiated, destroyed. And we agreed, I think, that this can happen. But surely it is much more common for change to occur in a piecemeal, evolutionary sort of way.

8. Hilary Putnam argues against "the tendency to think that if the absolute is unobtainable, then 'anything goes.'" He quotes John Austin who says that "*enough is enough, enough isn't everything*" (Hilary Putnam, *Realism with a Human Face* [Harvard University Press, 1990], p. 131).

We become acquainted with people from another culture and find things about them we admire. But we may not admire everything, and so we resist "conversion." We try to borrow what we think is good and incorporate that into our own way of life. Probably it won't come across exactly as it existed there, so it bends a bit, warps to fit. And in making it fit, other parts of our lives (or theories) change their shape, too. Our lives, and our cultures, too, are fluid in this way.

After all, we do learn. We learn about the world and come to have more and more adequate beliefs about it. We learn from others who are more knowledgeable or wiser. We can even learn better how to learn.

And we can learn that some standards are better than others.

ELIZABETH: Wasn't it precisely the slave-owner's *standards* that were bad? Our standards for who is to count as a full human being are clearly an improvement on his. If that isn't a rational judgment, I don't know what is. Any theory that would demote such a claim to the status of a "purely personal preference" *must* be mistaken.

MICHAEL: As a defender of modern science, I want to say that one thing we have learned is how to learn about the world better. And I think we have good reason to say so!

FRED: I've got to jump in here again. This just sounds like ethnocentrism all over again. From what point of view are you saying that our standards are *better* than others? Or that we now know *better* how to learn about the world than our ancestors did?

ANITA: From our own point of view, of course. But unless you are captured by this unrealistic picture you and Peter have constructed for us, it is a perfectly reasonable thing to say. Being rational, it seems to me, is basically a matter of *problem solving*. You've got a problem when something in your life is unsatisfactory. You are hungry and you don't like that. So you have to solve that problem, and you do it by finding something to eat. A perfectly rational procedure; and it is perfectly clear that your state after you eat is *better* than it was before.

Sometimes the unsatisfactory part of your life is a belief—or a scientific theory, or a state of society like slavery. So you strike out on a search for alternative beliefs or theories or forms of social life. And if you find them, and they work out, your life is better.

Sometimes the problem is that you don't have good learning skills, and you hunt around for better ones. Or it may be that your standards are not so good; they may make you a sucker for every fast-talking con-man or politician. That can be a problem—a *felt* problem.

PETER: But maybe it isn't felt. And that, I think, shows a "problem" with the view you are sketching. We find something unsatisfactory, as you put it, only because it conflicts with some *interest* we have. Suppose I don't have an interest in food? Or imagine that I don't want to avoid con-men. Then these "problems" won't be problems for me. And getting beyond them won't seem "better."

Your "problem-solving approach" falls right back into relativism. What counts as a "good solution" to a problem—what even counts as a *problem*—is relative to people's interests, to what they find satisfactory.

It's still the same old predicament.

ANITA: There are two replies to that. First of all, I think we *are* in a kind of predicament; but I don't think you relativists describe it correctly. The predicament we are actually in is one of never being absolutely certain that we have the truth, or the best line on how to live. Think about the law; it only requires that we prove a case beyond any reasonable doubt. And sometimes, when we have done that, we find out later that we made a mistake. But we may still have done our best at the time.

I think that is a good rule for life, as well. We have to give up hope of certainty. In this respect I agree with you and Fred; we could only get certainty if we could jump outside our own minds and compare our beliefs to bare, uninterpreted reality. And we can't do that. So we are stuck with our best guesses, with hypotheses, beliefs, theories, and standards we haven't yet found unsatisfactory. We go with what we've got until we find it no longer works for us. We're fallible through and through, and we just have to live with that.

ELIZABETH: I vaguely remember that this view has a name, too. It's called *fallibilism*.

MICHAEL: You talk like a pragmatist, Anita.

ANITA: I can accept both those descriptions. But my pragmatic fallibilism isn't relativism; at least not if relativism holds that every framework for belief is as good as any other, or that rationality is restricted to well-defined frameworks, or that radical cognitive change can only be non-rational. Problems sometimes get *solved*. We are not always hung out to dry between equally plausible alternatives.

And here we come to my second answer to Peter. Mike made the point earlier that humans have at least some basic interests in common. I agree with that and think it is important. I don't think these interests can include an interest in the *truth*, as Mike holds, unless you mean by "true" something like "works for us." But setting that aside, I want to add the claim that interests, too, can be better or worse. And that some interests are better than others is something we can learn.

FRED: I'd like to see an argument for that!

ANITA: As you said the first night, nothing easier. Take someone who has fallen into some sort of compulsive behavior—gambling, for instance. The compulsive gambler can correctly be described as having acquired one overriding interest; his passion for betting leads him to subordinate all his other interests to it. So he steals from his friends, embezzles from his employers, lies to his family, and neglects his children.

While he is in the grip of this interest, that will be the only thing that matters to him, and you won't be able to talk him out of it. (This may be one of those extreme cases where something like a conversion is required.) But it is beyond question that having a more balanced set of interests makes for a *better human life*.

So some interests are better than others.

FRED: So *you* say. But maybe not everyone would agree. The gambler in the grip of his mania probably wouldn't agree. Who's to say whether you or he is right?

ANITA: This is a commonly made point, but agreement doesn't make something so, and the lack of agreement doesn't mean it isn't so. When I say that X is better than Y, I don't *mean* that everyone agrees—or even that many do. So disagreement by itself can't refute the claim.

Such judgments may not be certain, and disagreement may well motivate us to look again at our convictions. But the sheer fact that not everyone agrees is no reason at all for giving up our considered judgments.

FRED: You say "better" doesn't mean "agreed to." Technically I suppose you are right. But then I think you owe us an account of what it *does* mean. My own view is that it can't mean more than "seems better to me," or maybe "seems better to my culture."

ELIZABETH: But that can't be right. When I am wondering what I should do in some perplexing situation, I am *not* wondering about what *seems* best to me. I may already know *that*. What I want to know is whether what seems best is really best. If "better" just meant "seems better to me," my concern would be nonsense. And it isn't nonsense.

SAM: And in situations like that *I* am not particularly interested in what seems best to my *culture* (if that can be identified). Even if I did know that, the question would still remain as to whether my culture had it *right* about the best thing to do.

FRED: Then you do owe us an explanation. When you say that our standards for treating fellow humans are better than those of the slave-traders, or when Mike says that our methods for learning about the world are better than the method of consulting the ancestors' words, just what *are* you saying?

ANITA: It is easier to exclude mistaken suggestions than to give a positive account. But if I had to make a stab at it, I would say something like this:
To say that X is better than Y is to say that it will *work* better for us, that X will satisfy our deepest interests more adequately than Y.

FRED: And what are our deepest interests?

ANITA: I can't tell you very precisely. But they have to do with a kind of ideal human life, with what might be called human flourishing.

I know that is pretty vague. But it clearly excludes slavery, in which neither master nor slave can flourish; slavery dehumanizes the slave and degrades the master. This is something we have learned, and we are better persons for it. I think feminism is making a significant contribution to it by showing that women aren't just a kind of afterthought, a second-best sort of human being, but whole and complete persons in the same sense that men are.

Our idea of human flourishing is fluid and dynamic. We can make mistakes here as everywhere, and we have no certainty that we are on the right track. But with all our fallibility, what we mean when we say one set of standards or practices is better than another is that it contributes to the flourishing of human beings—and it is reasonable to think so.

PETER: But you have to admit that not everybody has the same ideal of what it is to "flourish." For some it means obedience to God, or Allah, or a Buddhist denial of desire. For others it is a sensually rich and varied life. Some may seek a sense of calm well-being and an absence of chronic worry or fear. For still others, to flourish is to create or produce something of value.

ANITA: Yes, of course. And you will say that relativism gets a new foothold in the variety of ideals.

PETER: I will indeed!

ANITA: A harmless kind of relativity has to be allowed here. No, it must even be *insisted* on. Individuals differ from each other in all sorts of ways, and what permits one to flourish would stifle another. We need to be sensitive to varying capacities, talents, and temperaments. There are so many good things a person can do, from plumbing, to poetry, to parenting. I am certainly not suggesting that one narrow ideal of human flourishing should be imposed on people.

We have to allow that there can be *many* good forms of human life. But that a free society is better than a slave society, that a democracy is better than totalitarianism, that we are better people if we treat each other with respect and concern—all these things we have learned. They are part of human flourishing. And these things are *not* relative.

MICHAEL: How do you see this idea of human flourishing related to science?

ANITA: Let's see, what would I say about that? I think by and large modern science has contributed to the flourishing of humans, though not without exception. I guess I would say that the pursuit of science is justified only insofar as it does contribute. What I mean is that science isn't an end in itself. Suppose you are right that science is the best way we have of learning about the world; if we came to a point where it was pretty clear that more science would diminish human flourishing rather than encourage it, then I think we should refuse to do it. Doing science is subordinate to the ideal.

And I definitely do not think science provides the only sort of knowledge that is worth having. We can learn as much, perhaps more of real importance, from a study of biography, history, anthropology, and the law.

ELIZABETH: And from literature and the arts, as Peter suggested the other evening.

SAM: And from the Bible. I said before that science doesn't save souls. I don't think pragmatism does either.

ANITA: Well, I don't know about saving souls; what I'm interested in is a decent society in which individual men and women can live good, satisfying lives.

Mike said that science provides a powerful alternative to relativism. I think a broadly pragmatic outlook offers an even more plausible alternative, which includes all that can reasonably be said on behalf of science.

(*There is silence for a few minutes, as though they are all dazed by the variety and complexity of the arguments they have set out. Yet they seem reluctant to call it a night.*)

But Liz, you haven't said much on your own account. Except for a few remarks here and there, you have pretty much sat on the sideline, looking thoughtful.

ELIZABETH: This may surprise you, but I think I sympathize most with Sam.

FRED: With Sam? I thought he was odd man out here.

SAM: Frankly, so did I. But I am delighted to hear it.

ELIZABETH: As I listened to the arguments I kept thinking about Socrates—and my children.

ANITA: A strange combination!

ELIZABETH: Socrates says we will be better people if we search for things we don't know rather than despair of finding them.

FRED: What does old Soc mean by "better"?

ELIZABETH: He might not answer your question in just the sense you asked it, but I think he says we will be more courageous and less idle.[9] And I think that's a good answer—a good *kind* of answer.

Anita complained that Peter's description of our cognitive life was too abstract. But "better" is scarcely less abstract—to say nothing of the definitions for it that were proposed: "seems better to me," or "contributes to human flourishing." Even Anita had to admit that was pretty thin.

ANITA: But not entirely empty!

ELIZABETH: No. But I think Socrates' account brings us down to more concrete concepts. If you are told that a certain person is "not

9. Socrates says, "I would contend at all costs both in word and deed as far as I could that we will be better men, braver and less idle, if we believe that one must search for things one does not know, rather than if we believe that it is not possible to find out what we do not know and that we must not look for it." Plato, *Meno* (Hackett Publishing Co., 1980), 86b–c.

entirely a good man," you don't know very much. But if you learn that he is cowardly and lazy, you know a good bit. These words are full of content, thick with description, in a way that "good" and "bad" and "better" are not.

PETER: That may be so. But I am mystified about why you think it is important—or what connection it has with our discussion.

SAM: I confess I don't see it either, Liz. What's the relevance of this courage and idleness stuff?

ELIZABETH: Think about the line, "custom is king over all." Taken one way it just says human beings live very diverse lives and believe very different things. And that is certainly true, but neither very exciting nor profound.

But that sense slides into others which amount to a kind of counsel of despair. So we find ourselves saying that there's no telling what's *really* good or true. That maybe the notions of "absolutely good" or "objectively true" don't even make sense— that all we have are opinions, anyway. So who's to say? Maybe one opinion is as good as another. It all comes down to personal preference in the end anyway.

MICHAEL: I seem to be hearing echoes.

ELIZABETH: And in the end we are left with that miserable concept "true-for-me."

FRED: Hey! That's a favorite of mine.

ELIZABETH: But think how it originates, Fred. I hear it from my students when they are being pressed hard in argument. They try to escape this way and that, but nothing works. And finally they take refuge in "Well, anyway, it's true for me!"

FRED: What do you expect them to do?

ELIZABETH: I don't want to be too hard on them; they are still young. But they *could* admit defeat—say they were mistaken and have now learned something. Or they *could* say, "I don't see how to answer that right now; let me think about it and I'll get back to you." Or they *could* just admit their ignorance.

But "true-for-me" is the perfect defensive maneuver. It allows us to keep whatever belief we are fond of in a completely secure way. How could anyone show me that something I believe sincerely isn't true *for me*? Climbing back into that hole, I am completely safe.

Besides, there is something dishonest about the phrase. To try to hang on to the good odor of "true" while cutting out its heart with the qualifier—as Fred does when he says it simply means, "that's how I see it"—just smells bad.

MICHAEL: You are saying it's kind of a cowardly move.

ELIZABETH: Exactly. To venture out in public with what you think is *true* takes courage. You expose yourself. Not just your beliefs, but *yourself*, since *you* are the one who has accepted these beliefs. And that's scary.

But Socrates says we shouldn't be afraid to do that; we shouldn't be afraid to be shown wrong. He even says it is a great benefit to us if someone shows us we are mistaken—since having false opinions is an evil we should wish to be without.

PETER: That may sound good. But of course it makes sense only if there *is* such a thing as non-relative truth.

ELIZABETH: That's *true*, Peter.

PETER: . . . Wait a minute. That's not another one of those "reflexive cards" being played, is it?

ELIZABETH: I suppose it is. But my point is that when you make an unselfconscious remark like that—in this case one I agree with—you *commit* yourself to its correctness. And expose yourself to critique.

You *didn't* mean, did you, that it was only "true for you" that Socrates presupposes the non-relativity of truth? It didn't sound like it.

PETER: Hmmm. But for all we know, you *could* construct an interpretation of Socrates that denies he has a commitment to absolute truth. Then what I said would only be "true" relative to an interpretation I was, for the moment, taking for granted.

ELIZABETH: A good trick that would be! But Anita has the right reply here.

ANITA: That even if you could do it, there is no guarantee it would be as good an interpretation as its opposite. Some interpretations are *better* than others.

PETER: Relative to certain standards for evaluating goodness!

ANITA: Some of which are better than others!

MICHAEL: Back on the merry-go-round again. I want to know whether Liz has any way out of that circle. You said, Liz, we would be less lazy if we assume there is a truth to pursue.

ELIZABETH: Think back to what Peter said were the motivations lying behind his form of "non-dogmatic" relativism. He wants to avoid ethnocentric arrogance and contempt for other ways of life; he pleads for charitable openness to views radically different from our own. So far so good. But we can ask, to what end? He says that we can benefit from those exposures, and again I agree. But unless he means that we can *actually become better human beings* in specific and concrete ways, what does benefiting mean? And why should we go to the trouble, if things are as Peter believes?

The strategy Peter pursues of trying to show us that we are caught in a "relativistic predicament" undercuts the motivation he professes. For if there isn't any sense in which we could progress toward being *absolutely* better, what's the point? Peter's tack seems guaranteed to leave us complacent, satisfied with being what we are. Why, after all, should we open ourselves to other ways of life and belief if we *know* we can always say, "Well, that's your interpretation, right by your standards; but, sorry, I have my own"? Relativism takes away the risks, but in doing so takes away the benefits as well. It's a recipe for idleness for sure.

PETER: Maybe not. Maybe it's a way to make life more interesting.

ELIZABETH: That it may do. But if all we are talking about is the interesting, then I am content to let relativism have the day. If you find ancient Chinese vase painting interesting and I don't, then that's that. I may not understand what you see in it; but "to each his own" is the right motto here.

I thought we were talking about more serious matters—about virtues and vices, the morally good and the wicked, what makes a human life a really good one.

MICHAEL: And whether we can know the truth about the world.

ELIZABETH: And we surely can—partially, fallibly. But often with confidence, too. There may be all sorts of hard questions about what a human being is; theories in biology, psychology, and sociology may give tentative answers to those questions; but that David and I have produced two human beings is one certain truth about the world! Children are the best proof I know of for Mike's claim that we live in a world of independent realities.

SAM: You can say that again.

ELIZABETH: As I listened to our conversation, I kept wondering, what do I want for my children? What would I want them to believe? And when I think of that, I come back to those remarks of Sam's, that science doesn't save souls, nor does pragmatism. Nor, I would add, does relativism. Science just doesn't address the question; that's not its business, though when it gives us truths about the world—or even working theories—we should welcome them. Pragmatism, I think, settles for too little. And the relativist just gives up.

PETER: I think you had better tell us what this "saving of souls" is supposed to come to.

ELIZABETH: I think goodness, real goodness in human life, is rare and difficult. Most of us live in a kind of mediocre acceptability. I suppose we should be grateful, in this world filled with evil, for that much. But I want more.

At the heart of human life there lives the fat relentless ego—continually busy justifying its own works, interpreting everything in its own favor, making itself look good to itself and others.[10] I wonder whether it isn't the ego that lies behind the popularity of relativism. Arguments for relativism *appeal* to the ego; they make it look good – at least as good as any other ego!

I want to get beyond the comforting fantasy constructions of our selfishness. What I want for my children is that they be honest with themselves and others rather than deceptive, compassionate rather than indifferent, kind not cruel, wise and not foolish. What I want for them is to *love* – to care so much for others and the world they live in that they can see it for what it really is.

What I *don't* want is for them to learn that "it's all relative." I don't want them to ask "Who's to say?" when they face hard questions about the morally good thing to do. In that question you can just *see* the indifferent shrug of the shoulders. We don't need more handy excuses for self-indulgence.

There *is* an answer to the question, "Who's to say?" It shouldn't function as a merely rhetorical device. The correct answer is that *I* am to say, and *you*, and *we together* are to say. These questions about the good life are not ones we can shrug off this way. They *do* get answered one way or another. And if we don't do our best to answer them well, the lazy, the wicked, and the self-interested will answer them for us. Or we will become like them ourselves.

I don't often think in terms of "souls" at all. But I think I know what Sam means. If I were to try to answer Peter's question, I would say that "saved souls" are people who unbend from that cramped focus on themselves and – freed from the distortions of self-concern – forget themselves in caring attention to the "other" – whether world or person.

FRED: I didn't know you were a religious person, Liz.

ELIZABETH: Am I? I suppose I am in some sense. All I know is that a really good person would be impatient with so much in these discussions. I was the one who first suggested we talk about this topic; but more and more I am thinking that you don't sit around

10. "In the moral life the enemy is the fat relentless ego" (Iris Murdoch, *The Sovereignty of Good* [Routledge and Kegan Paul, 1970], p. 52).

and argue about the reality of lifeboats while the ship is sinking. You do the best you can to save the drowning—the best you *can see to do*.

The relativism debate presents itself as an attempt to determine the limits on our quest for truth and goodness, trying to discern what we are capable of attaining. But how do we know what we are capable of while we are still on the way, still participants in the struggle for the true and the good? Why should we let ourselves be distracted from the task of becoming as good and as wise as we can be?

You, Peter, rode your bike up every hill; I admire that. But what made it happen was your painful struggle—especially on the mountain today—not some speculation about whether you could do it or not. That's what I want in life, too. I want us to be challenged, stretched to our utmost, pulled away from self-satisfied contentment with our current selves toward the good.

PETER: But isn't it obvious that your idea of the good may not be that of another person?

ELIZABETH: We know enough about it to move in the right direction. Just as we know that our children exist, so we know that treating them cruelly is evil; that doubts about this are unreal was shown by Sam's example the first night. We know that indifference will leave us where we are, and will leave the evil in the world as it is. And we know that loving attention to the reality of others and of our situation is something good. Of course there's a lot that's unclear; and it's so hard to see through the self-produced fog of our illusions. So hard.

MICHAEL: This all sounds very personal, very private. We've been talking about confronting others who are different from ourselves— about ethnocentrism.

ELIZABETH: Being ethnocentric, I think, is just another way of being self-centered; it's just "we" instead of "me." It is just as hard to overcome. Maybe harder. But I don't think it can be countered satisfactorily by relativist tactics which play directly into the hands of the dear self. What we need is a respectful, unsentimental attention to the aspects of those lives that are strange to us. Caring about them, achieving some clarity about them, we may be able to find ways of living together which will enhance the goodness of us all.

ANITA: And perhaps enlarge and correct our own narrow versions of goodness and truth, too?

ELIZABETH: Sure. But if we were really in the skeptical position Peter tried to put us in, we wouldn't have any idea how to begin— what to borrow, what to modify, what to celebrate. I worry that relativism may *enhance* ethnocentrism rather than weaken it, leaving us smugly content with what we have, immune to any *real* challenge to its goodness and truth.

ANITA: There's a lot in what you say that I am sympathetic to. But you said pragmatism settles for too little. I don't think I will agree, but maybe you could say a bit more about what you mean.

ELIZABETH: Much of our life is well described by your picture of piecemeal problem-solving to find something that works, that satisfies. And you are right to emphasize that we can learn more satisfactory ways to learn, that we can acquire better standards and even improve somewhat the structure of our interests. These are all strategies for coping, for getting along in a reasonably satisfactory way. But coping just isn't enough.

I think your pragmatism is either *too complacent* or *too optimistic.* Either it leaves us too much where we are or it unrealistically assumes that by pragmatic methods we can solve our deepest problem. As far as I can see, you don't come to grips with the fact that there is something desperately wrong with us—our domination by the dear self and entanglement with its strategies for assuring that *I* always come out on top.

SAM: What Christians call sin. You are saying that you believe in sin and Anita doesn't.

ELIZABETH: Something like that, I suppose.

FRED: You are religious!

SAM: Do you believe in grace, too?

ELIZABETH: I don't know. I find it hard to talk about this sort of thing. All I know is that there is a kind of attraction to the good, something like a pull towards it which counters our selfishness. But I'm about at the end of what I can see here. Don't ask me more.

MICHAEL: I think we are all about at the end of our vision; it's gotten late tonight. Tomorrow is our last day together, and I want to say how great it has been to see you all again. And how much I have enjoyed our conversations.

PETER: And the rides.

ANITA: I have to say it, Peter. You were magnificent.

PETER: Actually, I thought so, too. I still don't think I'm defeated; but I confess that a lot of the things you all said here will rattle around in my brain for a long while. And who knows what the outcome will be?

MICHAEL: I dare say that's true for all of us.

ANITA: I have the feeling that as these conversations rattle around in *my* brain, some new questions will occur to me.

FRED: No doubt!

ELIZABETH: It's only fair if you, or any of us, have further questions that we should hear them. Why don't you write them down and send them around to us? Socrates wouldn't want us to stop thinking just because we're going home.

SAM: These five days have been such an excellent adventure that I think we should agree to do it again. Maybe we'll be surprised at what we become in the next ten years.

FRED: We may not have settled the question of whether custom is king over all. But I'd be happy if this event became a custom among us.

ELIZABETH: I'm for it. Though I will love seeing my family tomorrow, I wouldn't have missed this for the world.

MICHAEL: In another decade then. I wonder what the topic will be?

ANITA: At this point I can't look beyond tomorrow. And I am glad to say that the hard riding is over; it's all downhill from here. Goodnight all.

Further Reading

Though none of the characters in this dialogue is modeled on any one thinker, the reader may find it useful to have a brief guide to some sources for the arguments presented. Development of these ideas and arguments can be found in many other books as well.

Fred's first pattern of argument, in favor of individualist relativism, will probably be familiar to the reader from personal conversations. Its origin can be traced back to the views of Protagoras and some of the other "sophists" of ancient Greece. For a good discussion, see the relevant chapter in John Manley Robinson's *An Introduction to Early Greek Philosophy* (Houghton Mifflin Company, 1968). A more extensive treatment is G.B. Kerferd's *The Sophistic Movement* (Cambridge University Press, 1981). Plato presents a characterization of Protagoras in his rather difficult dialogue of that name.

His argument in the second conversation echoes presentations of cultural relativism. Classic sources are William Graham Sumner, *Folkways* (Ginn and Company, 1940, originally published in 1906) and Ruth Benedict's *Patterns of Culture* (Pelican Books, 1946)—especially chapter 7. A useful collection of essays on this topic is *Ethical Relativism*, edited by John Ladd (University Presses of America, 1985).

Peter's attempt at a "non-dogmatic relativism" is inspired by Paul Feyerabend's "Notes on Relativism," in his book *Farewell to Reason* (Verso, 1987). Some of Peter's arguments have sources in the classic literature of skepticism; see, for instance, Sextus Empiricus, *Outlines of Pyrrhonism* (Harvard University Press, 1955) and Michel de Montaigne, *Apology for Raymond Sebond* in *The Complete Works of Montaigne* (Stanford University Press, 1958). Recent literary criticism (deconstruction) inspired by Jacques Derrida and Michel Foucault also uses many of these arguments.

An accessible examination of Michael's defense of the objectivity of science is found in *Scientific Realism*, edited by Jarrett Leplin (University of California Press, 1984). For a look at relativist arguments (pro and con) pertaining to science, see the dialogue by Larry Laudan, *Science and Relativism* (University of Chicago Press, 1990). The recent critique of science as ideology serving certain interests can be surveyed in *Scientific Rationality: The Sociological Turn*, edited by James Robert Brown (D. Reidel Publishing Company, 1984).

Classic sources for Anita's pragmatic views are *Pragmatism*, by William James (Harvard University Press, 1978, first published in 1907) and John Dewey's *The Quest For Certainty* (Capricorn Books, 1960, originally published in 1929). An engaging presentation of this point of view can be found in certain essays of Hilary Putnam's recent book, *Realism with a Human Face* (Harvard University Press, 1990); look particularly at the essays in Part II, "Ethics and Aesthetics."

There are many presentations of Sam's views available, but the books of C. S. Lewis can perhaps be especially recommended. See, for example, *Mere Christianity* (Macmillan, 1986) and *The Screwtape Letters* (Macmillan, 1982). Classic sources are the works of Augustine, Thomas Aquinas, Martin Luther, and John Calvin. And, of course, there is *The Bible*.

Elizabeth cites Socrates, who is presented to us in Plato's dialogues. See especially *Euthyphro, Apology, Crito, Meno, Symposium,* and *Republic*, all published by Hackett Publishing Company. There are echoes of Søren Kierkegaard in what she says; see the sections in *Concluding Unscientific Postscript* (Princeton University Press, 1944) entitled "Something About Lessing," "The Task of Becoming Subjective," and "The Subjective Truth." See also *The Sovereignty of Good* by the novelist and philosopher Iris Murdoch (Routledge & Kegan Paul, 1970).